A CALL FOR JUSTICE:

An Assessment of Access to Counsel and Quality of Representation in Delinquency Proceedings

A Report of the American Bar Association Juvenile Justice Center, Juvenile Law Center, and Youth Law Center, with funding from the U.S. Department of Justice Office of Juvenile Justice and Delinquency Prevention

Photographs that appear in this document were produced independently, and bear no relationship to subjects or cases discussed in the text.

A CALL FOR JUSTICE:

An Assessment of Access to Counsel and Quality of Representation in Delinquency Proceedings

PREPARED BY:

Patricia Puritz, Project Director
American Bar Association Juvenile Justice Center

Sue Burrell, Youth Law Center
Robert Schwartz, Juvenile Law Center
Mark Soler, Youth Law Center
Loren Warboys, Youth Law Center

Reprinted
December, 2010

IN MEMORIAM

To Amelia Lewis for her compassion
and foresight in the representation of
Gerald Gault

1903–1994

Amelia Dietrich Lewis and Gerald Francis Gault

Viewpoints expressed herein are those of the authors and do not necessarily
represent the official position or policies of the Office of Juvenile Justice and
Delinquency Prevention, unless expressly stated.
This Report has not been approved by the House of Delegates
or the Board of Governors of the ABA.
© December, 1995

ISBN 1-57073-260-4

ADVISORY BOARD

Mary Broderick,
Executive Director
California Attorneys for Criminal
  Justice
Los Angeles, California

Paul DeMuro,
Consultant
Montclair, New Jersey

Barry C. Feld,
Centennial Professor of Law
University of Minnesota
  Law School
Minneapolis, Minnesota

Scott Harshbarger,
Attorney General
Commonwealth of Massachusetts
Boston, Massachusetts

Randy Hertz,
Director
Juvenile Rights Clinic
New York University School of
  Law
New York, New York

Jane Knitzer,
National Center for Children
  in Poverty
Columbia University
New York, New York

Barry Alan Krisberg,
President
National Council on Crime
  and Delinquency
San Francisco, California

Alice A. Lytle,
Judge
Sacramento Municipal Court
Sacramento, California

Orlando L. Martinez,
Consultant
Martinez and Associates
Highlands Ranch, Colorado

David Mitchell,
Judge
Circuit Court for Baltimore
Baltimore, Maryland

Andrew J. Shookhoff,
Judge
Juvenile Court of Davidson
  County
Nashville, Tennessee

Charles Z. Smith,
Justice
Washington State Supreme Court
Olympia, Washington

Robert Spangenberg,
Director
The Spangenberg Group
Boston, Massachusetts

Randolph N. Stone,
Director
Mandel Legal Aid Clinic
University of Chicago Law School
Chicago, Illinois

Jo-Ann Wallace,
Director
Public Defender Service
Washington, DC

TECHNICAL CONSULTANTS

Robert J. Baughman,
Executive Director
Coalition for Juvenile Justice
Washington, D.C.

Marty Beyer,
Consultant
Great Falls, Virginia

James W. Brown,
Director
Community Research
  Associates
Champaign, Illinois

Earl L. Dunlap,
Executive Director
National Juvenile Detention
  Association
Richmond, Kentucky

Barbara Danziger Flicker,
Consultant
Beverly Hills, California

Richard Gable,
Director of Applied Research
National Center for Juvenile
  Justice
Pittsburgh, Pennsylvania

Geoff Gallas,
Executive Administrator
First Judicial District of
  Pennsylvania
Philadelphia, Pennsylvania

James R. Irving, Assistant
  Warden (Ret.) Sheridan
  Correctional Center Aurora,
  Illinois

David A. Kozlowski,
Attorney
Legal Services of South Central
  Tennessee
Tullahoma, Tennessee

Patricia A. Lee,
Attorney
Office of the San Francisco
  Public Defender
San Francisco, California

Frank Orlando,
Director
Center for the Study of Youth
  Policy
Fort Lauderdale, Florida

Robert Shepherd,
Professor of Law
T.C. Williams School of Law
University of Richmond
Richmond, Virginia

TABLE OF CONTENTS

Acknowledgements		xi
Foreword		xiii
Executive Summary		3
Preface		15
Chapter One:	Access to Counsel and Quality of Representation - A Review of the Literature	19
Chapter Two:	The Role of Defense Counsel in Delinquency Proceedings	29
Chapter Three:	Assessment Results	41
Chapter Four:	Promising Approaches to Effective Representation	59
Chapter Five:	Recommendations and Implementation Strategies	67
Endnotes		73

ACKNOWLEDGEMENTS

This project would have been impossible without the involvement of the hundreds of juvenile defenders who took the time to respond to a lengthy survey, and the scores of lawyers, judges, young people, social workers, prosecutors, court administrators and others who agreed to share their personal views through in-depth, on-site interviews. To them we are grateful.

In addition to a dedicated advisory board and impressive roster of technical consultants, some individuals deserve special recognition for their invaluable contributions, especially: Marty Beyer, Michael Dale, Barry Feld, Julie Glynn, Randy Hertz, Bridget McCormack, and Susan Hillenbrand.

We are also indebted to many people all over the country who contributed to our understanding of the problems juvenile defenders face and helped to shape the contours of this report. Special thanks goes to: James Bell, Bart Lubow, Catherine Ross, Barbara Smith, and Shannan Wilber, and to our grant monitors at the Office of Juvenile Justice and Delinquency Prevention, Betty Chemers and Douglas Dodge.

And, of course, there would be no report were it not for the tireless behind-the-scenes work of the staff, paralegals and interns of our organizations, including: Merete Felch-Pederson, Lisa Gindy, Kenneth Goldsmith, Jesse Goldstine, Matthew Logan, Wendy Shang, Aaron Sheppard, Jeff Shook, and especially Alyssa Logan of the American Bar Association Juvenile Justice Center; Tabitha Abu El-Haj, Kate Greenwood, and Beth Tomlinson of the Juvenile Law Center; and Susan Ludi, Nicole Manganaro, and Stephanie Morris of the Youth Law Center. Their dedication and good humor made it all come together.

Our collective work is dedicated to the young people who become embroiled in the juvenile justice system, the defenders who serve them, and our unwavering belief that these youth are worth fighting for.

The Authors
December, 1995

FOREWORD

I am pleased to present to you *"A Call for Justice: An Assessment of Access to Counsel and Quality of Representation in Delinquency Proceedings."* This report was commissioned by the Office of Juvenile Justice and Delinquency Prevention in response to the 1992 amendments to the Juvenile Justice and Delinquency Prevention Act.

I have long believed that our most meaningful attempts at both rehabilitation and prevention must be targeted at our youth. We have much work to do, however, to guarantee that our juvenile justice system is responsive and nurturing, promotes accountability for one's actions, and recognizes the need to provide for public safety. The defense bar is at the heart of ensuring that the system which seeks those goals operates as fairly, accurately and humanely as possible.

This comprehensive assessment of the state of delinquency defense services comes at a propitious time. The need for access to quality defense attorneys for juveniles has never been greater. There is a strong movement in the country to increase the sanctions for juvenile offenders. Because there are more numerous and harsher consequences for acts of delinquency, defense attorneys are an important buffer against unfairness. Good lawyers get good information to judges and prosecutors. Every child accused of crime needs a zealous representative to ensure that courts have the "right" juvenile before them, and that decisions from pre-trial detention to post-trial disposition and beyond are made with all the facts necessary for balanced decision-making.

This report was drafted by an experienced team, led by the Juvenile Justice Center of the American Bar Association, with a group of veteran juvenile justice experts from the Youth Law Center and Juvenile Law Center.

In many ways the recommendations contained in this report are simple. Reduce caseloads. Increase training and resources. Ensure that attorneys begin a case early and stay with their clients until they leave the system. Implementation, however, will not be so easy. It will require the cooperation and energy of state and local bar associations, juvenile court judges, and state and local officials. Such cooperation is essential if we are to provide justice for juveniles.

Shay Bilchik
Administrator
Office of Juvenile Justice and Delinquency Prevention

Executive Summary

EXECUTIVE SUMMARY

I've been to court three times already and I just want to get it over with. I'm scared and I don't know if they're going to send me to jail. I don't know who my lawyer is. He wasn't there when the judge called my case.[1]
—Jose R., charged with possession of stolen property

Jose's lawyer, a public defender assigned to represent him, has over 500 other cases. On an average day he has 10 to 15 cases on several court calendars. Some days he cannot get to each courtroom because there is not enough time. On those days his cases are called, but he is not there to represent his clients. Jose's lawyer is a committed, creative and talented attorney, but he can't possibly keep up with his caseload.

Jose's anxiety and confusion are common among children in juvenile court. So is his lawyer's dilemma: too many cases, too few resources, not enough hours in the day. The result, increasingly, is a lack of basic fairness for young people charged with delinquent acts.[2]

In the United States today, the juvenile justice system is at the center of public debate. The public is concerned about juvenile crime, particularly violent crime.[3] Despite the fact that fewer than one-half of one percent of juveniles in the United States were arrested for a violent offense in 1992, Congress, state legislatures, and executive agencies have insisted that the juvenile courts respond with more punitive sanctions, longer periods of confinement for many youthful offenders, and increased handling of juveniles in adult criminal court.[4]

These measures have important consequences for youth in juvenile court as well as for society at large. Youth face the prospect of much longer sentences, mandatory minimum sentences, and time in adult jails or prisons. This is so, even though most juveniles in custody have committed non-violent offenses and only a small percentage of juvenile offenders will become career criminals as adults.[5] Confined youth are likely to find overcrowding and other dangerous conditions: about half of all confined juveniles are in facilities that exceed their design capacity, and many facilities have substantial deficiencies in the areas of security, education, management of suicidal behavior, and health care.[6]

These trends are likely to exacerbate the pervasive disproportionate representation of nonwhite youth in the juvenile justice system. State studies reveal that nonwhite youths are at even greater disadvantage than their white counterparts at several, if not all, stages of representation. Nonwhite youths are not only overrepresented in the system, they are also treated more harshly. In some states, nonwhite youths are more likely to be detained, and more likely to be locked up, than white youths charged with similar offenses.[7]

For society at large, there are also important interests at stake. Increased incarceration will require state and local governments to commit hundreds

Despite the high stakes involved in today's juvenile court proceedings, many children still fail to receive effective legal representation. In some jurisdictions, children regularly appear in delinquency proceedings with no attorney at all.

of millions of dollars to build more juvenile facilities, at a time when state and local budgets are already severely stretched. Consequently, it is critically important to use secure detention (before adjudication) and institutional confinement (after adjudication) only for those serious and violent young offenders who truly need to be removed from our communities, and to develop effective community-based programs for youth who do not need incarceration. In addition, it is counterproductive to lock up nonviolent youth with violent offenders or place them in other conditions that are likely to lead them to more violent behavior.

The role of counsel is central to these considerations. Young people charged with delinquency offenses need effective representation to ensure that they are not held unnecessarily in secure detention, improperly transferred to adult criminal court, or inappropriately committed to institutional confinement. They need the active assistance of counsel to properly challenge prosecution evidence and to present evidence in their behalf. If the charges against them are sustained, they need effective representation to assure that the dispositional order is fair and appropriate to their individual needs. If they are incarcerated, they need access to attorneys to help respond to a myriad of post-dispositional legal issues.

Society also needs well-trained and knowledgeable counsel to ensure that expensive institutional resources are reserved for those youth who truly need them, and that young people receive the services they need to avoid future trouble, as well as to provide equal justice in adversarial proceedings.

The U.S. Supreme Court recognized children's constitutional right to counsel in delinquency proceedings in its 1967 decision, In re Gault.[8] Yet despite the high stakes involved in today's juvenile court proceedings, many children still fail to receive effective legal representation. In some jurisdictions, children regularly appear in delinquency proceedings with no attorney at all.

In the fall of 1993, the American Bar Association Juvenile Justice Center, in conjunction with the Youth Law Center and Juvenile Law Center, received funding from the federal Office of Juvenile Justice and Delinquency Prevention to initiate the Due Process Advocacy Project. The intent of the project is to build the capacity and effectiveness of juvenile defenders through increasing *access* to lawyers for young people in delinquency proceedings and enhancing the *quality* of representation those lawyers provide. This report does not address the significant number of young people now being handled by adult criminal courts.

This project, called for by Congress in 1992 in its reauthorization of the Juvenile Justice and Delinquency Prevention Act, has even greater importance today. The juvenile justice system in our country is at the center of public debate. The public is concerned about juvenile crime, particularly violent crime. Congress, state legislatures, and executive agencies have insisted that the juvenile courts respond with more punitive sanctions, longer periods of confinement for many youthful offenders, and increased handling of juveniles in adult criminal courts.

These measures have important consequences for youth in juvenile court who need effective representation to ensure that they are not held unnecessarily in secure detention, improperly transferred to adult criminal court, or inappropriately committed to institutional confinement. Society at large also has important interests at stake, including the desire for appropriate and effective sanctions for juvenile offenders and the enormous costs of increased incarceration and building new juvenile facilities at a time when state and local budgets are already severely stretched.

This report is a national assessment of the current state of representation of youth in juvenile court and an evaluation of training, support, and other needs of practitioners. The assessment sought information about excellent work being done in the field as well as problems in representation of youth. It examines all stages of representation, from the time of arrest to the time of discharge from the juvenile justice system, and covers all regions of the country, including urban, suburban, and rural areas.

THE ASSESSMENT

The assessment consisted of a national survey of hundreds of juvenile defenders, site visits to a variety of jurisdictions, interviews with people working in the field, client interviews, an extensive literature search, and meetings and consultation with the project's national Advisory Board. The assessment focused on public defenders and court-appointed counsel. We also examined the small but important role played by law school clinical programs and non-profit children's law centers. We compared our observations with the Juvenile Justice Standards developed by the Institute for Judicial Administration and the American Bar Association.

ACCESS TO COUNSEL AND QUALITY OF REPRESENTATION

In 1967, in *In re Gault*, the United States Supreme Court established a constitutional right for children to receive counsel in juvenile delinquency proceedings. Congress expressed similar concern over the need to safeguard children's rights when it enacted the Juvenile Justice and Delinquency Prevention Act in 1974. When it reauthorized the Juvenile Justice Act in 1992, Congress re-emphasized the importance of lawyers in juvenile delinquency proceedings, specifically noting the inadequacies of prosecutorial and public defender offices to provide individualized justice. In a 1993 report, *America's Children at Risk: A National Agenda for Legal Action*, the ABA's Presidential Working Group on the Unmet Legal Needs of Children and their Families also called for the juvenile justice system to fulfill children's right to competent counsel.

During the past fifteen years, a number of researchers have described and analyzed the difficulties of children in many jurisdictions in ob-

Many of the problems that plague the juvenile justice system—including appalling conditions in confinement, inappropriate transfer to adult court, overrepresentation of children of color, and inadequate health and educational services—could be remedied if every child accused of a crime was well represented by competent counsel, knowledgeable about juvenile justice issues...
America's Children at Risk: A National Agenda for Legal Action, 1993.

taining access to counsel. Others have raised serious concerns about the quality of representation when children are represented by attorneys. Some studies have taken in-depth looks at particular states, such as Minnesota and New York, while others have examined systemic problems. Commentators have noted a variety of barriers to appropriate access to counsel (including parental reluctance to retain attorneys, judicial hostility to appointment of counsel, and improper "waivers" of counsel by juveniles) and to effective representation by attorneys (such as inadequate training, high turnover, low status of juvenile court work, and insufficient support services). Overwhelming caseloads for many juvenile defenders impede both access to counsel and quality of representation.

THE ROLE OF DEFENSE COUNSEL IN DELINQUENCY PROCEEDINGS

The right to representation by counsel is not a formality. It is not a grudging gesture to a ritualistic requirement. It is of the essence of justice.
Kent v. United States 383 U.S. 541, 561 (1966)

The job of the juvenile defense attorney is enormous. In addition to all of the responsibilities involved in presenting the criminal case, juvenile defenders must also gather information regarding clients' individual histories, families, schooling, and community ties, in order to assist courts in diverting appropriate cases, preventing unnecessary pre-trial detention, avoiding unnecessary transfers to adult court, and ordering individualized dispositions. Juvenile defenders have an important role in protecting their clients' interests at every stage of the proceedings, from arrest and detention to pretrial proceedings, from adjudication to disposition to post-dispositional matters.

The assessment sought to evaluate how effectively attorneys in juvenile court are fulfilling their obligations to their clients.

ASSESSMENT RESULTS

We observed many attorneys who vigorously and enthusiastically represented their young clients. Those lawyers challenged the prosecution to prove its case through pertinent evidentiary objections, motions, arguments, and contested hearings. In court, they were articulate and prepared. Their arguments were supported with relevant facts and law. When their clients were faced with lengthy incarceration, they often provided the court with compelling alternatives. The children they represented appeared to understand the proceedings. There was ongoing communication between children and their attorneys, both in and out of court. The attorneys made good use of family members, other significant adults, experts, and potential service providers to demonstrate to the court the appropriateness of non-institutional placements.

But this type of vigorous representation was not widespread, or even very common. Often what we were told in interviews and what was reported in mail survey responses did not square with what we personally observed in courtrooms and detention centers. The assessment raised serious concerns that the interests of many young people in juvenile court are significantly compromised, and that many children are literally left defenseless.

Our intent is not to blame the many dedicated attorneys who are handling extremely difficult cases and laboring under tremendous systemic burdens. Rather, we want to highlight their problems and needs in order to build their capacity and support their ability to provide improved legal services to children and youth.

General Characteristics of Offices and Programs Surveyed

More than half of the public defender offices surveyed have at least some attorneys working exclusively on juvenile cases. In most of the offices, public defenders rotate from other courts to juvenile court, with the option of continuing to work there. In other offices, attorneys must rotate to adult criminal court in order to be promoted. Many public defenders do not stay in juvenile court very long. Among survey respondents, 55% stay less than 24 months.

Public defenders carry enormous caseloads. While caseloads varied, the average caseload carried by a public defender often exceeds 500 cases per year, and of that number, greater than 300 are juvenile cases.

Most appointed counsel who represent children in juvenile court are solo practitioners or in small firms. Their experience in law practice ranged from two years to twenty, and in juvenile court from less than one year to more than five. Their caseloads are much less than public defenders: a significant number carry under 50 cases, though approximately one-fifth carry more than 200 cases. Only about one-third handled more than 75 juvenile delinquency cases during the year preceding the survey.

Attorneys in law school clinical programs and children's law centers, whom we also surveyed, typically carry very small caseloads.

Public defenders carry enormous caseloads. While caseloads varied, the average caseload carried by a public defender often exceeds 500 cases per year, and of that number, greater than 300 are juvenile cases.

Waiver of Counsel

One of the most disturbing findings of the assessment is that large numbers of youth across the country appear in juvenile court without lawyers: for example, 34% of the public defender offices surveyed reported that some percentage of youth in the juvenile courts in which they work "waive" their right to counsel at the detention hearing. Reports by appointed counsel are very similar.

These waivers occur after an advisory colloquy in the presence of the judge slightly more than half the time (54%), but 46% of the public defenders say there is a colloquy only "sometimes" or "rarely." In addition, 45% of public defenders say the colloquy is only "sometimes" or "rarely" as thorough as that given to adult defendants and is often a meaningless technicality.

Waivers of counsel by young people are sometimes induced by suggestions that lawyers are not needed because no serious dispositional

Waivers of counsel by young people are sometimes induced by suggestions that lawyers are not needed because no serious dispositional consequences are anticipated — or by parental concerns that they will have to pay for any counsel that is appointed. These circumstances raise the possibility — perhaps the likelihood — that a substantial number of juvenile waivers are not "knowing and intelligent."

consequences are anticipated — or by parental concerns that they will have to pay for any counsel that is appointed. These circumstances raise the possibility — perhaps the likelihood — that a substantial number of juvenile waivers are not "knowing and intelligent."

Impact of High Caseloads

The assessment found high caseloads to be the single most important barrier to effective representation. High caseloads have an impact on many aspects of representation. Attorneys with heavy caseload burdens find it difficult to meet with young clients to explain the proceedings before they appear at their detention hearings, conduct thorough investigations of the circumstances of the alleged offenses, learn about youths' ties to their families and to their communities, research and write individualized pretrial motions, keep informed on community-based alternatives to secure detention, develop dispositional plans that may be preferable to institutional confinement, follow up with clients during dispositional reviews, or monitor placement problems that may arise regarding needed services or conditions of confinement.

High caseloads plagued public defenders everywhere. Almost none of the public defender offices surveyed have a cap on the number of juvenile cases they may handle. More than two-thirds of public defenders feel that caseload pressures limit their ability to represent juvenile clients effectively. More than a third of those responding said that the time available to meet with and prepare clients before their cases are called is inadequate. In addition, almost half say that the time they have to confer with clients after their case is called is inadequate.

Appointed counsel reported fewer such problems. However, for appointed counsel carrying 200 or more cases, the impact on representation was similar to that experienced by public defenders with similarly high caseloads.

Site visits revealed the problem in more detail. At several sites, children literally met their lawyers as they sat down at counsel table in the detention hearings. There was no time to investigate the charges or to obtain information from families, schools, or social service agencies. At several sites, probation officers reported that juveniles do not know who their lawyers are or what the charges are.

The impact of all this on youth in juvenile court is devastating. Children represented by overworked attorneys receive the clear impression that their attorneys do not care about them and are not going to make any effort on their behalf. One youngster said that his hearing "went like a conveyor belt."

High caseloads have a debilitating impact on attorneys as well. Burnout, job dissatisfaction, and anxiety over never having enough time to do a complete job are serious problems for many caring juvenile defense attorneys. Ultimately, the results are likely to be secure detention of youth who pose no significant danger to themselves or others, reduction in the accuracy of judicial decision-making, unnecessary transfers of juveniles to the adult system, dispositions that have little connection to public safety or children's needs, and a denial of fundamental fairness.

Appointment of Counsel

It is critical that counsel appear early in the life of the case. At first appearances in court, if judges ask about the events surrounding alleged offenses, the circumstances of arrests, the roles of other youth involved, or clients' prior contacts with the juvenile justice system, and attorneys do not have answers, they lose the initial opportunity to present clients' cases in a favorable light. Judges are left to review the uncontradicted allegations in the charging petitions. Based on incomplete reviews, judges make early determinations regarding detention that may influence cases all the way until their dispositions.

Despite the importance of early and aggressive lawyering, many public defenders and court-appointed counsel do not even meet with their clients until the proceedings have begun. Indeed, many public defenders and private counsel are not appointed until the detention hearing, and in many locations, a single attorney handles most detention hearings and accepts the appointment of counsel for a panel of attorneys, then cases are sent "downtown" for proper assignment of counsel later on, delaying the beginning of actual representation for many days.

Children represented by overworked attorneys receive the clear impression that their attorneys do not care about them and are not going to make any effort on their behalf. One youngster said that his hearing "went like a conveyor belt."

Pretrial Preparation and Trial Performance

Inquiries into pretrial motions practice and trial performance yielded important information about a number of barriers to effective representation. High caseloads again create problems. Attorneys who barely have time to cover all of their cases on a particular day do not have the time or energy to research and write effective pretrial motions. The inadequacy (or absence) of training is another serious problem, as is lack of professional supports such as specialized texts, computerized legal research, access to paralegals, availability of bilingual staff or translators, and adequate space for interviewing and meeting with clients.

In addition, courthouse culture deters many attorneys from filing motions or aggressively pursuing sound defenses at trial. In many juvenile courts there is a high premium placed on "going along" and "getting along." Many judges frown on defense attorneys who take on adversarial roles.

In addition, courthouse culture deters many attorneys from filing motions or aggressively pursuing sound defenses at trial. In many juvenile courts there is a high premium placed on "going along" and "getting along." Many judges frown on defense attorneys who take on adversarial roles.

Disposition

Most attorneys responding to the survey reported that they can adequately prepare for disposition. At the site visits, however, a very different picture emerged: many attorneys openly acknowledged that their representation is deficient at the dispositional phase. The main reasons cited were the lack of time to keep up with placement options and other dispositional alternatives for the client, lack of time to prepare adequate dispositional plans, and an overall lack of alternatives in the system itself.

As at the other stages of representation, high caseloads make it difficult, if not impossible, for public defenders to provide effective representation at dispositions. The problem is compounded by the lack of resources and support services.

These findings are of serious concern, particularly because dispositional hearings are often the last and most important opportunity for counsel to protect their clients' interests. Although some attorneys provide excellent representation — with social workers available to conduct client evaluations and prepare individualized dispositional plans — many are unable to provide judges with any alternatives to the recommendations of probation officers.

Post-Dispositional Representation

An alarming aspect of juvenile defense is the infrequency with which appeals are taken.

An alarming aspect of juvenile defense is the infrequency with which appeals are taken. Public defenders rarely take appeals in juvenile cases. Among public defender offices responding to the survey, 32% are not even authorized to handle appeals. Of the offices that do handle appeals, 46% took no appeals in juvenile cases during the year prior to the survey.

Appointed lawyers also take appeals rarely. Among the appointed lawyers surveyed, three-quarters were authorized to handle appeals but four out of five took none during the prior year.

Among the public defenders surveyed, almost one-third usually end their representation at the dispositional hearing. Post-dispositional review hearings can result in release or relocation of juveniles, and afford opportunities for the court to learn what is really taking place inside juvenile justice programs. Nevertheless, many defense attorneys do not view their role at such hearings as particularly "useful."

Of those public defender offices that do represent youth at post-dispositional reviews, three-fourths usually interview the youth before the hearing, but only a little over half usually review the treatment plans and interview probation or parole officers before the review hearing. Fewer than one-third of the attorney respondents usually interview treatment staff, investigate alternative placements, or monitor implementation of treatment plans for juveniles in placement.

About forty percent of the appointed lawyers surveyed end their representation after the dispositional hearing. Those who continue to provide representation at post-dispositional review hearings generally do more than public defenders— high percentages usually interview the child before the review hearing; interview probation or parole officers before the hearing; review the treatment plan; interview the child's family; and investigate alternative placements before the hearing. However, fewer than a quarter often monitor the implementation of their clients' treatment plans.

Training and Support Services

There are serious gaps in the training available to juvenile defenders: seventy-eight percent of public defender offices do not have a budget for lawyers to attend training programs; about half do not have a training program for all new attorneys, do not have an ongoing training program, and do not have a section in the office training manual devoted to juvenile delinquency practice. About forty percent do not have a specialized manual for juvenile court lawyers, and about a third do not include juvenile delinquency work in the general training program, do not have any training manual, and do not have a training unit.

Moreover, there are significant gaps in the topics covered in public defender trainings: three-quarters of the offices do not cover pretrial motions practice; two-thirds do not cover transfer of juveniles to adult court; three out of five do not cover client-specific dispositions or detention alternatives; over half do not cover child development and issues of capacity, and half do not cover how to show amenability to treatment. Juvenile defenders repeatedly told us that they need additional training on dispositional alternatives, funding mechanisms, and working with related systems such as special education.

Similarly, only 38% of the appointed lawyers reported the availability of a criminal law training program for representing indigent juvenile defendants.

Attorneys at a number of sites voiced a need for staff social workers to assist in client needs assessment and alternative disposition plans. Others spoke of the need for basic secretarial support, investigators, paralegals, and computers. Amazingly, at one site the lawyers did not even have the very basics of law practice - desks, telephones, files, or offices. They just used the bare counsel table in the courtroom, with the judge and court clerk present, to conduct their business.

More than half of the public defender offices do not have bilingual attorneys available to communicate directly with clients who speak the first most commonly spoken language other than English, and a quarter of the offices do not have any translators available for clients who speak the first most commonly spoken language other than English.

Despite conspicuous omissions, there were some sites that had very positive training programs, many of which could be emulated elsewhere. Some offices provided extensive training prior to assigning cases to lawyers; others had creative training mechanisms such as mentoring by experienced attorneys, brown bag lunches on current juvenile justice issues, or the provision of a yearly training "allowance" per attorney.

Promising Approaches to Effective Representation

While the assessment revealed substantial deficiencies in access to counsel and the quality of representation in juvenile court, it would be incorrect to conclude that effective representation of young people cannot and does not exist. Project staff observed many individual de-

While the assessment revealed substantial deficiencies in access to counsel and the quality of representation in juvenile court, it would be incorrect to conclude that effective representation of young people cannot and does not exist.

fenders around the country who were delivering first-rate legal services to their young clients. Defender programs that appear to be of high quality have a number of characteristics in common:

- Supportive structural features of the program that make effective representation possible, including limitations on caseloads, the ability to enter the case early on, and the flexibility to represent the client in related collateral matters (such as special education);
- Comprehensive initial and ongoing training, and available resource materials;
- Adequate non-lawyer support and resources;
- Hands-on supervision of attorneys;
- A work environment that values and nurtures juvenile court practice.

The negative impact of caseload pressures at every stage of the delinquency process cannot be overstated. Some defender offices have attempted to address this problem internally, by allowing attorneys to ask for temporary relief from new case assignments if their caseload is too burdensome. Other offices provide juvenile representation through a team approach, involving social workers and investigators, as well as lawyers.

RECOMMENDATIONS AND IMPLEMENTATION STRATEGIES

Chapter Five of this report sets forth in detail a comprehensive set of recommendations and implementation strategies.

REPORT

PREFACE

In the fall of 1993, the American Bar Association Juvenile Justice Center, in conjunction with the Youth Law Center and Juvenile Law Center, received funding from the federal Office of Juvenile Justice and Delinquency Prevention to initiate the Due Process Advocacy Project. The intent of the project is to build the capacity and effectiveness of juvenile defenders through increasing access to lawyers for young people in delinquency proceedings, and enhancing the quality of representation those lawyers provide. This report does not address the significant number of young people now being handled by adult criminal courts.

The project began with a national assessment of the current state of representation of youth in juvenile court and an evaluation of training, support, and other needs of practitioners. The assessment sought information about excellent work being done in the field as well as problems in representation of youth. It examined all stages of representation, from the time of arrest to the time of discharge from the juvenile justice system. It covered all regions of the country, including urban, suburban, and rural areas, to permit development of appropriate strategies for improving representation in a range of community settings.

The assessment consisted of a national survey of juvenile defenders, site visits to a variety of jurisdictions, interviews with people working in the field, client interviews, an extensive literature search, and meetings and consultation with the project's national Advisory Board.

Project staff mailed the survey to public defender offices and court-appointed lawyers throughout the country, law schools with clinical programs that handle juvenile delinquency cases, and specialized children's law centers that exist in a number of communities.[9] We received responses from 124 public defender offices handling juvenile delinquency cases, 56 court-appointed attorneys, 24 law school clinical programs, and 24 children's law centers.

The survey provides the first systematic national assessment of current practices of juvenile defenders. Since the surveys asked for information about entire offices rather than individuals, the collection of information profiles the experiences of a large number of the men and women who represent young people in juvenile court across the country.

The surveys[10] covered a broad range of issues, including:

- Characteristics of the office or program;
- Number of juvenile cases handled during the previous fiscal year and the impact caseload size has on the program's ability to represent juveniles effectively;

The survey provides the first systematic national assessment of current practices of juvenile defenders. Since the surveys asked for information about entire offices rather than individuals, the collection of information profiles the experiences of a large number of the men and women who represent young people in juvenile court across the country.

- The number of juveniles who waive the right to counsel and the circumstances under which such waivers occur in the jurisdiction;
- Duration of representation;
- The nature of attorney-client interaction during various stages of representation;
- The scope of appointment of counsel in (a) delinquency cases, (b) related, non-delinquency cases, (c) disposition review hearings, and (d) appellate proceedings;
- The availability of various types of training for juvenile defenders and the adequacy of the available training;
- The availability and adequacy of library resources and support services for juvenile defenders;
- The ability of juvenile defenders to communicate with non-English speaking clients;
- The level of resources available to juvenile defenders compared with prosecutors;
- The most significant factors that hinder the ability of defense attorneys to provide full representation to juvenile clients; and
- Resources and support services that would improve the quality of defense services provided to juveniles.

In addition to the surveys, project staff visited ten jurisdictions across the country, including urban, suburban, and rural settings. Staff interviewed judges, defense attorneys, prosecutors, clients, court administrators, and youth advocates. Staff observed client interviews and detention, adjudication, and disposition hearings. Staff also visited detention centers and juvenile correctional facilities. When the site visits were completed, staff discussed their findings with the project's Advisory Board and with technical consultants assisting on the project.

Assessing access to representation was reasonably straightforward. For the purposes of this project, representation begins when an attorney first meets with a juvenile client, and ends when an attorney no longer has responsibility for protecting a client's interests. If an attorney is assigned or appointed to represent a young person, representation may also begin with an initial interview of the client by an attorney's paralegal, investigator, or law student intern.

Although the six attorneys who conducted the national assessment have extensive experience in the juvenile justice field, assessing quality of representation was more subjective and more difficult. We felt the best available objective measures of quality of representation were the Juvenile Justice Standards developed by the Institute for Judicial Administration and the American Bar Association.[11] The twenty volumes of Juvenile Justice Standards have been American Bar Association policy since 1980. The Standards set minimum guidelines for all stages of the juvenile justice process and include specific standards for representation of minors in juvenile court. We used the Standards to help formulate the survey questions and to conduct the site evaluations.

In addition, the project's Advisory Board and technical consultants are composed of nationally-recognized legal scholars, juvenile court and appellate judges, public defenders, law school clinical professors, public officials, juvenile justice researchers, policymakers, criminologists, and juvenile corrections administrators. Their involvement helped immeasurably to conduct the assessment and analyze the results.

Chapter One of this report reviews the literature on access to counsel and quality of representation. Chapter Two is an overview of the delinquency process and the role of defense counsel in delinquency proceedings. It examines the role counsel can and should play at each major stage of a delinquency case. Chapter Three focuses on the assessment results, comparing and contrasting the mail surveys and the information gathered at the site visits. Chapter Four describes characteristics of promising approaches to effective representation, including the role of law school clinical programs and nonprofit children's law centers. Chapter Five sets out the recommendations for improving the current quality of juvenile defense work. The tear-off sheet at the end of the report lists items in the appendix which are available upon request.

CHAPTER 1

ACCESS TO COUNSEL AND QUALITY OF REPRESENTATION A REVIEW OF LITERATURE

It has been more than twenty-five years since *In re Gault*[12] highlighted the mistreatment of children within the justice system and established the constitutional right of children to appointed counsel in juvenile delinquency proceedings. In a landmark opinion that remains the standard for children's due process rights, Justice Fortas announced that "[u]nder our Constitution, the condition of being a boy does not justify a kangaroo court."[13]

In establishing a constitutional right to appointed counsel for children, the Supreme Court rejected arguments that the probation officer or the juvenile court itself could appropriately represent a child. Given the "awesome prospect" of incarceration up to the age of majority, the Court found that an accused delinquent is entitled to an attorney "to make skilled inquiry into the facts, to insist upon the regularity of the proceedings, and to ascertain whether he has a defense and to prepare and submit it."[14] In addressing the argument that bringing lawyers into juvenile proceedings would destroy the informality of the proceedings, the Court turned to the Report of the President's Commission on Law Enforcement and the Administration of Justice, *The Challenge of Crime in a Free Society* (1967):

> Informality is often abused. The juvenile courts deal with cases in which facts are disputed and in which, therefore, rules of evidence, confrontation of witnesses, and other adversary procedures are called for. . . . [J]uveniles often need the same safeguards that are granted to adults. And in all cases children need advocates to speak for them and guard their interests, particularly when important decisions are made. It is the disposition stage at which the opportunity arises to offer individualized treatment plans, and in which the danger inheres that the court's coercive power will be applied without adequate knowledge of the circumstances.
>
> Fears have also been expressed that the formality that lawyers would bring into juvenile court would defeat the therapeutic aims of the court. But informality has no necessary connection with therapy . . .[15]

Congress expressed similar concern over the need to safeguard children's rights when it enacted the Juvenile Justice and

> "Under our Constitution, the condition of being a boy does not justify a kangaroo court. The traditional ideas of Juvenile Court procedure, indeed, contemplated that time would be available and care would be used to establish precisely what the juvenile did and why he did it..."
>
> *In re Gault,*
> 387 U.S. 1, 28 (1967)

Delinquency Prevention Act (JJDPA) in 1974.[16] The Congressional statement of findings specifically observed that "understaffed, overcrowded juvenile courts, probation services, and correctional facilities are not able to provide individualized justice or effective help."[17] The JJDPA created the National Advisory Committee for Juvenile Justice and Delinquency Prevention (NAC) to develop national juvenile justice standards. The resulting Standards for the Administration of Juvenile Justice[18] required that children be represented by counsel in all proceedings arising from a delinquency action, beginning at the earliest stage of the decisional process.[19] In 1980, the Institute for Judicial Administration/American Bar Association (IJA/ABA), Joint Commission on Juvenile Justice Standards also promulgated extensive standards calling for representation of children in all stages of delinquency proceedings and defining the role of counsel.[20]

When Congress reauthorized the JJDPA in 1992, it re-emphasized the importance of lawyers in juvenile delinquency proceedings.

When Congress reauthorized the JJDPA in 1992, it re-emphasized the importance of lawyers in juvenile delinquency proceedings. The "Congressional Findings and Declaration of Purpose" in the reauthorization specifically noted the inadequacies of prosecutorial and public defender offices to provide individualized justice or effective assistance. Moreover, Congress added that a purpose of the Act is "to assist State and local governments in improving the administration of justice and services for juveniles who enter the system."

The American Bar Association's Presidential Working Group on the Unmet Legal Needs of Children and Their Families has also called for the juvenile justice system to fulfill children's right to competent counsel. In its 1993 report, *America's Children at Risk: A National Agenda for Legal Action*, the Working Group decried the fact that many thousands of children each year are adjudicated delinquent and incarcerated in facilities resembling jails or prisons, without the benefit of counsel, and that among those who have counsel, many are represented by lawyers untrained in the complexities of representing children.[21] The Working Group found that many of the problems that plague the juvenile justice system, including appalling conditions of confinement, inappropriate transfer to adult court, overrepresentation of nonwhites in the juvenile justice system, and inadequate health and educational services, could be remedied if children were represented by competent counsel at all points in the juvenile justice process, including the post-dispositional stage.[22] The report set forth an agenda for meeting children's right to counsel by developing more competent juvenile court attorneys. The report made it clear that the ethical obligations of counsel for children require attention to broader issues such as excessive detention of children; conditions of confinement in juvenile facilities; enforcement of federal laws such as the Juvenile Justice and Delinquency Prevention Act; racial bias in the juvenile justice system; treatment of status offenders, mentally ill children, and undocumented youth; transfer of children to adult court; and imposition of the death penalty on youth under the age of 18.[23]

ACCESS TO COUNSEL

Despite the directive of the Supreme Court in *Gault* and the JJDPA's acknowledgement of effective legal representation as a cornerstone of the juvenile justice system, a large number of children in this country still appear in court without a lawyer. The most extensive work to date on children's access to counsel is by Professor Barry Feld at the University of Minnesota Law School.[24] Feld has estimated that prior to *Gault*, attorneys appeared on behalf of children in perhaps 5% of juvenile delinquency cases.[25] Through his own analysis of data from six states, gathered from the National Juvenile Court Data Archive, Feld found that some states (or jurisdictions within states) still fail to appoint counsel in a majority of cases.[26]

In his analysis of other studies on access to counsel, Feld reported wildly varying representation rates in different parts of individual states. For example, lawyer appointment rates ranged from 19% to 95% in different counties in Minnesota.[27] Feld traced some of these disparities to differences in practices for appointment of counsel among urban, suburban, and rural areas.[28] He also noted that, while there is a positive correlation between the seriousness of the offense[29] and the appointment of counsel, serious offenses comprise only a small part of most juvenile court dockets. Thus, children accused of minor misbehavior are most likely to be incarcerated without the assistance of counsel.[30] Moreover, a 1986 study of access to counsel in Minnesota revealed that nearly one-third of all youths removed from their homes and more than one-quarter of those confined in state juvenile correctional institutions lacked representation at the time of their adjudication and disposition.[31] Studies from other jurisdictions have confirmed Feld's findings that access to counsel remains a serious problem.[32] Other studies have suggested that counsel is still not present during certain stages of the proceedings.[33]

> *"The juvenile needs the assistance of counsel to cope with problems of law, to make skilled inquiry into the facts, to insist upon regularity of the proceedings, and to ascertain whether he has a defense and to prepare and submit it."*
>
> In re Gault,
> 387 U.S. 1, 36 (1967)

John Arms

Researchers have found that in some jurisdictions the assistance of counsel is technically available, but children must formally request the appointment of an attorney. Frequently this does not happen. In addition, judges and court personnel may implicitly discourage children from requesting counsel in cases in which they anticipate that only a probationary term will be imposed. Not surprisingly, children in such jurisdictions often misunderstand their rights and fail to exercise them.[34] There has also been some study of status offenders, who may suffer serious consequences as a result of court jurisdiction but do not have the same right to counsel as delinquents under *Gault* or state law.[35]

Feld has suggested that low rates of representation are a function of inadequate public defender services (especially in rural areas); parental reluctance to retain an attorney[36] or to accept the appointment of a public defender, sometimes because the county may seek reimbursement for attorney's fees; judicial encouragement of waivers of counsel to ease the administrative burdens of the court; judicial hostility toward lawyers; judicial predeterminations not to appoint counsel in cases where probation is the anticipated outcome; cursory and misleading judicial advisories that inadequately convey the importance of the right to counsel and suggest that the waiver litany is a meaningless technicality; and waiver of counsel by children who truly do not understand their rights or what they are giving up in a "knowing and intelligent" way.[37]

In addition, the ABA Working Group on the Unmet Legal Needs of Children reported that children who are unrepresented may be unable to communicate important information that might affect decisions by judges and prosecutors. Without counsel, children often waive their constitutional rights without knowing the implications, and they are unable to pursue preadjudication motions and investigation that could have a profound impact on the outcome of the case. Further, unrepresented children may be confined for long periods or in deplorable conditions without an advocate to challenge the legal issues relating to jurisdiction, the conditions of custody, or adequacy of services.[38]

QUALITY OF REPRESENTATION

Even in jurisdictions where lawyers are appointed to represent children, there are strong grounds for concern about the quality of representation. Feld has suggested that public defenders for children are often neophytes who receive less training than their prosecutorial counterparts, and that appointed lawyers may be more concerned with maintaining ongoing relationships with the judges who appoint them than with protecting interests of their clients. Feld has argued that there is a particular need for lawyers to be better advocates in relation to dispositional alternatives; his research has shown that even fewer lawyers appear at dispositional hearings than at adjudicatory hearings.[39]

The most comprehensive study on the quality of juvenile representation is *Law Guardians in New York State: A Study of the Legal*

Representation of Children (1984), by Jane Knitzer and Professor Merril Sobie. The authors examined the quality of representation offered by law guardians in New York state by means of a multi-pronged research strategy.[40] As a result of their study, Knitzer and Sobie were able to present an unprecedented profile of the panel lawyers who represent children in New York courts.[41]

Knitzer and Sobie found that only one-quarter of the panel lawyers viewed themselves as juvenile law specialists. Over half of the panel lawyers reported that they had little interest in the substance of juvenile law. Nearly 70% indicated that they had no special screening, orientation, or co-counsel experience prior to joining the panel, and 30% to 40% had no relevant clinical or academic experience. Moreover, 42% of law guardians had no relevant training within the previous two years, with an even higher percentage of guardians in rural areas reporting no recent training.[42] The study found that under 15% of the panel attorneys handling juvenile delinquency and Persons In Need of Supervision cases viewed their role as analogous to that of a defense attorney. A substantial number of guardians reported that they were uncertain of their role. As a group, the guardians voiced a desire for training on current case law and legislation. They also felt a need for access to independent social workers and mental health professionals. Half of them, particularly those in rural areas, wished for access to a brief bank and paralegal assistance.

The self-reported inadequacies in training, experience, definition of role, and access to supportive services were confirmed by the authors' site visits, reports from others in the system, and document analysis. Overall, using the most basic criteria of effectiveness, 45% of the attorneys provided either seriously inadequate or marginally adequate representation; 27% were acceptable, and only 4% provided effective representation. In 5% of the cases it was clear that the lawyer had not met with the client; in 37% observers could not tell whether the lawyer had met with the client; and in 35% of the cases the lawyer did not talk to or had only minimal contact with their client during the court proceedings. In 47% of the observed cases it appeared that the law guardian had not prepared or had prepared only minimally for the case. In only a small percentage of cases did the law guardians appear to argue effectively in their clients' behalf or to be responsive to their clients during the proceedings. In only 35% of cases where the child had prior court contact with the system did the same law guardian provide representation in subsequent proceedings.

Knitzer and Sobie found that, apart from the effect of inadequate preparation, a very large number of cases had violations of statutory or due process rights that were left unchallenged by law guardians (almost 50% of the transcripts included appealable errors). Substantial numbers of guardians appeared unfamiliar with the governing law, and many assumed an inactive role in dispositional proceedings. Many had only perfunctory relationships with their child clients. The study found that law guardians seldom appealed court rulings, thus leaving bad rulings intact and issues demanding clarification unresolved.

> "Departures from established principles of due process have frequently resulted not in enlightened procedure, but in arbitrariness."
>
> *In re Gault,*
> *387 U.S. 1, 18–19 (1967)*

SYSTEMIC BARRIERS TO EFFECTIVE REPRESENTATION

In her 1983 monograph, *Providing Counsel for Accused Juveniles* (part of the Institute of Judicial Administration Current Policy Issues series), Barbara Flicker focused on organizational and fiscal considerations that affect quality of representation in various systems for providing counsel (public defender, legal aid societies, court-appointed counsel, contract/retainer systems). She found, for example, that many juvenile public defender systems suffer from underfunding, low morale, high turnover, lack of training, low status in "career ladders," political pressure, low salaries and huge caseloads. Effective representation in court-appointed counsel programs was impeded by other factors, such as the appointment of unqualified, inexperienced attorneys; inadequate monitoring of performance; and problems in maintaining independence from the judiciary that appoints the lawyers. With respect to contract or retainer systems, Flicker observed that cost-cutting measures such as flat fees for cases pose a serious threat to effective representation of delinquent children.[43] Studies of specific jurisdictions have also expressed concern about systemic barriers such as high caseload, underfunding, and lack of training for juvenile defenders.[44]

Judge Leonard P. Edwards has corroborated, from first-hand experience, many of Flicker's concerns about systemic impediments to effective representation.[45] As the presiding juvenile court judge in a large California metropolitan area, Judge Edwards noted that advocacy for children frequently loses out in the competition for scarce public dollars. Budget constraints result in high caseloads which, in turn, leave children's lawyers with insufficient time to investigate and prepare

their cases. In Judge Edwards' opinion, children's attorneys often have the least experience, and the lowest status in the legal community. Within public defender offices, the representation of children is typically considered less important than the "real work" of the office in representing adult felony clients, and career ladders are quite limited for juvenile court attorneys. Assignment to juvenile court is thought of as training before a promotion to felony trials, and the assignment of senior trial lawyers to juvenile work is considered punishment. Court-appointed panel attorneys are also less experienced and trained than their criminal court counterparts, and they, too, suffer from lower pay and status in the legal community. This results in a prevailing attitude that representing children demands less skill and care, less time and energy, and should be used as a stepping stone to more important work at the first opportunity. In Judge Edwards' view, the high turnover rate for juvenile court practitioners, pervasive lack of experience and training, and absence of commitment to representing children, combined with the inadequate allocation of fiscal resources, have had a significant, direct effect on the quality of representation of children.[46]

OVERWORKED AND UNDERSTAFFED: PRACTITIONERS' VIEWS

A poignant series of accounts from public defenders assigned to the juvenile court in Cook County, Illinois, confirmed much of what Flicker and Edwards reported with respect to public attorney offices. The accounts revealed that in some delinquency courtrooms attorneys handled more than 450 cases per year, even though the National Advisory Commission on Criminal Justice Standards and Goals recommends that public defender caseloads not exceed 200 cases per year. Lawyers may have 15 cases set for trial on one day, or 40 to 50 cases on calendar for a day. One public defender described the caseload as "mind-numbing." The attorneys reported that their caseload caused serious problems for them in preparing adequately for trial: one attorney reported that clients sometimes could not be interviewed at arraignment, and that interviews took place in a crowded hallway, only minutes before trial.[47]

Professor Janet Ainsworth performed a telephone survey of urban public defender offices and found no offices with juvenile court caseloads within recommended guidelines of 200 or fewer cases per year. Actual caseload per attorney in 1989 ranged from 250 to 550. There were suggestions that the situation was even worse in rural areas; other research indicated that one rural Washington county assigned 912 cases to one lawyer.[48] Similarly, M.A. Bortner's study of a metropolitan juvenile court revealed that public defenders handled some 80 to 90 cases per month.[49] Reports from other jurisdictions have echoed these concerns.[50]

> "The indispensable elements of due process are first, a tribunal with jurisdiction; second, notice of a hearing to the proper parties; and finally, a fair hearing. All three must be present if we are to treat the child as an individual human being and not to revert, in spite of good intentions, to the more primitive days when he was treated as a chattel."
>
> In re Gault, 387 U.S. 1, 19 (1967)

INADEQUATE PREPARATION AS A BARRIER TO ADEQUATE REPRESENTATION

Other writers have suggested that children's rights are violated not only by counsels' failure to understand their own role, but also by a failure to advise young clients properly, and to prepare their cases adequately. Richard A. Lawrence found that 17% of attorneys surveyed spent less than one hour on each case, 44% one to two hours, 28% three to four hours, and 11% five or more hours. He urged that the earlier appointment of counsel would reduce the wide variation in the quality of legal counsel and the amount of time that attorneys spend in preparation.[51] Similarly, M.A. Bortner found that for non-detained children, pre-hearing interviews with the child and families ranged from only thirty minutes to an hour, and that public defender actions were often based largely on a "paper profile" of the child and past experiences with court personnel as to what would be considered appropriate.[52]

ETHICAL CONFUSION AS A BARRIER TO QUALITY REPRESENTATION

Other commentators have focused on inadequacy of representation stemming from a failure to clearly delineate the role of juvenile counsel. Professor Robert E. Shepherd, Jr., and Adrienne Volenik have suggested that many of those who represent children do not understand their ethical obligations, and as a result, fail to zealously represent their young clients.[53] Thus, juvenile court attorneys are often uncertain whether to accede to the expectations of the court, the child's parents, or the child.[54]

It has been suggested that some lawyers fail to raise legitimate legal claims, fail to notify clients of their right to appeal, or even solicit *harsher* sentences for their young clients, believing that such actions are in their clients' best interests in the long run.[55] In her analysis of the IJA/ABA Standards for representation of children, Jan Costello described the ways attorneys for children have tacitly assumed the roles of other court personnel and essentially conceded the state's right to intervene.[56] This desire to "help" children, sometimes at the expense of good legal claims, reflects profound confusion about the lawyer's ethical duty to juvenile clients. Although ethical and legal standards call for attorneys to represent children as zealously as they would adults, the lingering strains of *parens patriae* ideology sometimes cause children's attorneys to abandon adversarial efforts in paternalistic deference to the court's efforts to intervene in the child's life.[57]

CHILDREN'S PERCEPTIONS OF BARRIERS TO EFFECTIVE REPRESENTATION

The consumers of juvenile court services, delinquent children, have focused on more concrete issues: communication problems and feelings of mistrust about their lawyer's commitment to them. Some of these problems may stem from insufficient preparation time, but others suggest more serious failures in relating to young clients. In a survey of 24 Colorado youth about their perceptions of the juvenile justice system, 34% had positive experiences with their attorneys, 53% had negative experiences, and 14% remained neutral on the subject.[58] Many of those reporting negative experiences felt that their attorney had given up, would not explain what was happening, would not tell the judge what the youth wanted, and was not on the youth's side. Many of the youth suggested that more time was needed with their lawyer to build trust, to enable their lawyer to know them as people, to be listened to, to share important information about themselves and the case, and to help them better process all the information flowing around the courtroom.

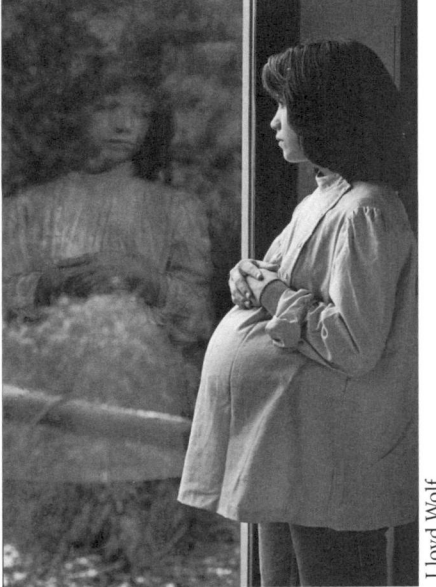

COMPROMISE AS AN IMPEDIMENT TO EFFECTIVE ADVOCACY

The caseloads carried by everyone in the juvenile court system have had other undesirable effects upon effective advocacy for children. A number of writers have commented on the institutional pressure for juvenile defense attorneys to cooperate in maintaining a smoothly functioning court system, sometimes at the expense of their clients' legal interests.[59] In some courts, attorneys are subtly reminded by the court, the prosecutor, and other court personnel that zealous advocacy is considered inappropriate and counter-productive. Lawyers who refuse to temper their advocacy to fit the prevailing comfort zone may suffer from subtle disapproval or more direct attacks, such as fee reductions or being excluded from the panel of court-appointed attorneys.[60]

CONCLUSION

Past studies have documented the ineffectiveness of juvenile representation in a number of locations. The intention of the survey and site visits summarized in the forthcoming chapters is to broaden the inquiry of past investigations to include nationwide information on public defenders, appointed attorneys, clinics and law centers, capturing what they do well and identifying what steps could be taken to enhance their work on behalf of juveniles.

CHAPTER 2

THE ROLE OF DEFENSE COUNSEL IN DELINQUENCY PROCEEDINGS

I've never been to court before. The judge says I can get a lawyer, but should I really talk to him? How do I know if I can trust him? Why should I believe he's really gonna help me? I don't know what to do.
—Xavier M., 14 year-old charged with auto theft

This section of the report discusses the major stages of a delinquency case and the role of counsel at each stage. Although there are many different approaches that a juvenile defense attorney needs to take at different stages of the proceedings, throughout the case counsel's role remains that of an advocate for the client's interests, as expressed by that client.

This discussion is an overview. It does not purport to cover in depth every aspect of representation of juveniles charged with delinquency.[61] Rather, it illustrates the processes and complexities of representation in juvenile court, and demonstrates the ways in which high caseloads, inadequate resources, and substandard practice deprive young people of effective representation.

Gault specifically stated that juveniles facing delinquency proceedings have the right to counsel under the Due Process Clause of the United States Constitution. The introduction of advocates for children theoretically altered the tenor of delinquency cases: juveniles accused of delinquent acts were to become participants in the proceedings, rather than spectators. *Gault* recognized that juveniles facing "the awesome prospect of incarceration" need counsel for the same reasons that adults facing criminal charges need counsel.[62] Thus, attorneys representing juveniles charged with delinquency must be prepared to assist clients to "cope with problems of law, to make skilled inquiry into the facts, to insist upon regularity of the proceedings, and to ascertain whether [the client] . . . has a defense and to prepare and submit it."[63] *Gault* recognized that a system in which the children's interests are not protected is a system that violates due process.

The job of the juvenile defense attorney is enormous. In addition to all of the responsibilities involved in presenting the criminal case, juvenile defenders must prepare "social" cases in order to assist courts in making dispositions. Attorneys must be aware of the strengths and needs of their juvenile clients and their clients' families, communities,

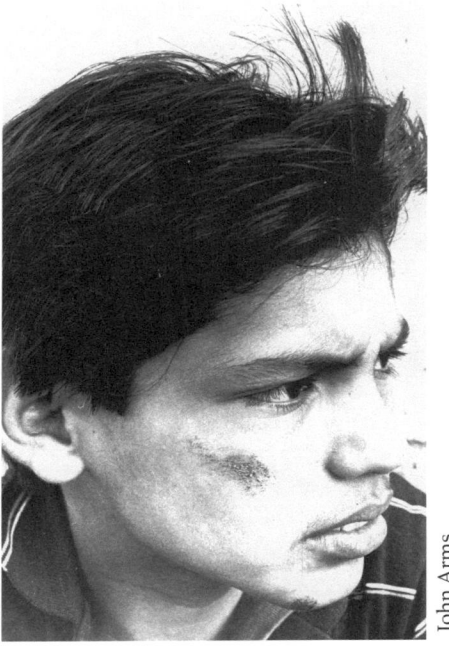

John Arms

"Due process of law is the primary and indispensable foundation of individual freedom. It is the basic and essential term in the social compact which defines the rights of the individual and delimits the powers which the state may exercise."
In re Gault,
387 U.S. 1, 20 (1967)

and other social structures, and must work with their clients to present information that will lead to appropriate services and community supports and, in some cases, out-of-home placements.

In order to be effective, both in meeting charges against clients and in dealing with social and family issues, juvenile defenders must establish good relationships with their clients. This takes considerable time and effort. Young people charged with crimes are often distrustful of adults, including their own attorneys. Counsel must patiently explain and emphasize that what clients tell them is confidential. Attorneys must build relationships with clients that will enable them to share deeply personal information.[64]

It is also vital that defenders take time to keep clients informed before and after court appearances and other significant events. Going through the system can be a confusing and frightening process. Young people often have incorrect notions of what might happen to them. Clients should be told exactly how to get in touch with counsel and when their attorney will next be in contact. Clients should be advised of what to do if rearrested and what their responsibilities are between court appearances.

ARREST AND DETENTION

I got arrested yesterday and today we went to court. I didn't get to say nothing. Nobody from my family was there. The judge kept me locked up. I don't know what will happen next.
        —*Lisa S., 15-year-old charged with gun possession*

Arrest is the point of entrance into the juvenile justice system. Sometimes that entry can be short-lived; in 1992 approximately one-third of juveniles arrested[65] were released by police due to insufficient evidence or "informal adjustment."[66] If the police determine that a case should proceed, the juvenile is usually either given a court date and released or sent to a detention facility. If sent to a detention facility, generally an intake officer decides whether to hold the child. If the juvenile is held, a detention hearing must occur within a time limit set by statute. It is often at the detention hearing that juvenile clients first meet their attorneys.

For youth not detained, the first meeting with their attorney may instead be at initial court appearances. That is not because there is no role for counsel earlier in the process. In fact, early intervention by lawyers—to investigate the charges, provide legal advice, and explore alternatives to secure detention—may have a significant impact on the entire course of delinquency proceedings.

Getting arrested can be frightening, especially if children are detained. By the time youths meet their attorneys, they may have been questioned by many adults, including police officers, intake workers, or family members. Additional adult questioning may be viewed by youths with distrust. Counsel must take the time to explain that their job is to help their clients defend against the charges. In addition to asking for information, it is vital that counsel take the time to discuss with clients what is likely to happen in court. The IJA/ABA Juvenile Justice Standards provide that during the initial stages of representation:

> Many important rights of clients involved in juvenile court proceedings can be protected only by prompt advice and action. The lawyers should immediately inform clients of their rights and pursue any investigatory or procedural steps necessary to protection of their clients' interests.[67]

At detention hearings, judges should review all information available about current alleged offenses, any past adjudications, any prior failures to appear in court, family and other community ties, school

Getting arrested can be frightening, especially if children are detained. By the time youths meet their attorneys, they may have been questioned by many adults, including police officers, intake workers, or family members. Additional adult questioning may be viewed by youths with distrust.

Lloyd Wolf

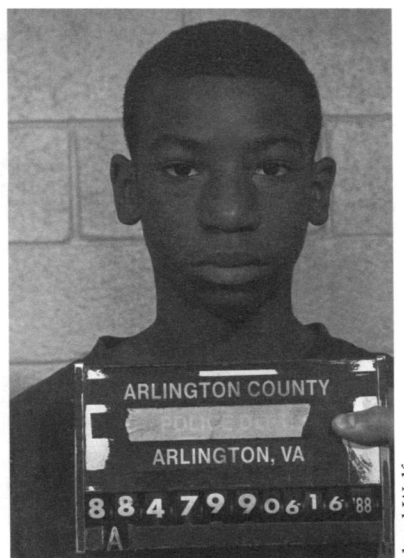

records, and any other information that may be relevant. Attorneys should argue that detention should only be used for young people who are dangerous or demonstrably likely not to appear. A minister, teacher, relative, or other mentor who comes to the detention hearing to offer to provide extra guidance and/or positive activities for the young person can make a big difference when the judge is considering detaining a non-dangerous youth because of lack of family supervision or truancy. Attorneys should make sure that judges have all the necessary information that would help their clients get released or placed in the most appropriate and least restrictive setting.

Effective representation and advocacy at the earliest stage of the proceedings may have a significant influence on the ultimate disposition of the case. Juveniles who are securely detained prior to adjudication—rather than released to parents or placed in community-based programs—are much more likely to be incarcerated at disposition than youth who have not been detained, regardless of the charges against them.[68] Thus, it is vital that defenders explore alternatives to secure detention as early as possible. The alternatives to secure detention may be quite varied and diverse, including group homes, residential treatment facilities, house arrest or other non-secure community-based programs.

Many juveniles waive counsel at the detention hearing and admit the allegations, following a brief (and often poorly-understood) colloquy with the court. Waiver of counsel by juveniles has been widely criticized. The IJA/ABA Juvenile Justice Standards specifically state that "a juvenile's right to counsel may not be waived."[69]

PRETRIAL PROCEEDINGS

It's better for my clients if I don't make a stink about their cases. Judges don't like it when you file motions. Anyway, most of them get probation.
— *Juvenile defense attorney*

"We made clear in that [Gault] decision that civil labels and good intentions do not themselves obviate the need for criminal due process safeguards in juvenile courts . . . "
In re Winship,
397 U.S. 358, 365–366 (1970)

Attorneys' work during the pretrial period of juvenile cases is critical to obtaining favorable outcomes for their clients. It is during this time that attorneys must investigate the facts, obtain discovery from prosecutors, acquire additional information about their clients' personal histories, file motions on behalf of their clients, and advocate for clients at probable cause hearings and other pretrial hearings. This stage of the case sets the foundation for strategies at adjudication hearings, negotiations with prosecutors, and development of appropriate dispositions.

At the pretrial stage, lawyers representing young clients must confer with them, according to the IJA/ABA Juvenile Justice Standards, "without delay and as often as necessary to ascertain relevant facts and matters of defense known to the client."[70] Counsel should begin investigating the charges as soon as possible, since it is at the early stage of cases that investigation is usually most fruitful. Early on, clients have

Lloyd Wolf

the freshest memories of the incidents as well as leads to find witnesses and ideas for defense strategies. Similarly, witnesses are easier to locate and have clearer recollections of the events in question. The IJA/ABA Juvenile Justice Standards stress the duty of lawyers to conduct a prompt investigation of the facts and circumstances of the case, and to obtain information in the possession of prosecutors, police, school authorities, probation officers, and child welfare personnel.[71] Lawyers should also explore "social or legal dispositional alternatives"[72] and investigate resources and services available in the community.[73]

Pretrial motions may be crucial to defense efforts, and there are benefits to filing motions even when they are denied. The prosecutions' written responses and testimony given at hearings on motions may provide valuable discovery material. "Locking" witnesses into their pretrial testimony may be helpful in preparing for trials. Filing clearly meritorious pretrial motions can also strengthen clients' positions for negotiating favorable dispositions.

There may also be other pending proceedings related to their clients' delinquency cases. These include, for example, school suspension hearings or probation revocations due to the conduct charged in the petitions. If possible, counsel should represent their clients at collateral hearings.[74] Such representation may be a useful tool for gathering information about the delinquency matters. It may also strengthen attorney-client relationships when clients see the extent to which counsel is committed to protecting their interests.[75]

As is true at the arrest and detention stage, during the pretrial process there is a great danger of lost opportunities to provide effective representation. The pressure of high caseloads, or the distant location of detention facilities, can make it difficult for counsel to meet

"Whether it is a minor or an adult who stands accused, the lawyer is the one person to whom society as a whole looks as the protector of the legal rights of that person in his dealings with the police and the courts."

Fare v. Michael C.,
442 U.S. 707, 719 (1979)

with clients, establish good relationships, learn more about clients' families, conduct effective investigations, file pretrial motions, and consider appropriate dispositions. Overburdened defenders may rely on information from the prosecutors to assess cases, or may simply have no time for motions practice. Detained clients may have limited contact with their attorneys, and may feel abandoned and become hostile.

TRANSFER AND AUTOMATIC WAIVER TO ADULT CRIMINAL COURT

What's happening? I'm scared to go to adult jail. My uncle and brother got shanked by a gang in there. They might come after me too.
—Lucien C., 14-year-old charged with armed robbery and waived to adult court

"But we are told that this boy was advised of his constitutional rights before he signed the confession and that, knowing them, he nevertheless confessed. That assumes, however, that a boy of fifteen, without aid of counsel, would have a full appreciation of that advice and that on the facts of this record he had a freedom of choice. We cannot indulge those assumptions."

Haley v. Ohio,
332 U.S. 596, 601 (1948)

In certain circumstances, juveniles may be prosecuted in adult criminal court. In the past, this was reserved for extraordinary cases in which chronic and serious young offenders had demonstrated that they would not benefit from the rehabilitative services and programs available in the juvenile court. Statutes often specified a small number of the most serious crimes for which juveniles could be prosecuted as adults, and often reserved such situations for older juveniles.

In recent years, however, as concern about juvenile crime has escalated throughout the country, many states have responded by enacting legislation to automatically prosecute more juveniles in adult criminal court. This has been accomplished primarily by statutorily increasing the number of offenses for which juveniles may be prosecuted in adult court, or by lowering the minimum age at which juveniles may be prosecuted as adults.

The traditional and still most common means to effect such prosecution for younger juveniles has been through "transfer" hearings in juvenile court. The hearings are also called "waiver" hearings, since the jurisdiction of the juvenile court may be "waived." At a hearing, the prosecution typically must make out a prima facie case—similar to proving "probable cause"—that the youth committed a crime that warrants transfer, and then must present evidence that the youth is not "amenable to treatment" in the juvenile justice system.[76]

In some states, the process is a "reverse transfer," in which juveniles charged with certain offenses are presumed *not* to be amenable to treatment, and the juveniles must demonstrate at hearings in adult court that they would benefit from being transferred to the juvenile court. In still other jurisdictions, the law simply gives prosecutors the discretion to decide whether or not youths charged with particular offenses will be charged as adults.

The consequences of transfer are enormous for clients. In many states, as soon as judges order transfers to adult courts, youths are moved from juvenile detention facilities and sent to county jails. If convicted in adult court, youths may be sentenced to jail or prison and housed with adult inmates. In other states, transferred youth may be sentenced to "youthful offender" institutions in which they are housed with older juveniles and young adults.[77] Although some states allow transferred youth to be placed in juvenile institutions,[78] they are the exception rather than the rule.

At transfer and reverse transfer hearings, counsel should argue that although the offense is serious, the young person is still a child, would benefit from services in the juvenile system, has not had sufficient opportunity to be rehabilitated, would likely be harmed in the adult system, and that the community could be protected from the young person during treatment as a juvenile. To make an amenability argument, counsel should, at a minimum: (1) describe the youth's background, including attachment to family and positive statements from individuals who believe that he/she has potential; (2) show that the young person was not thinking as an adult at the time of the offense; (3) describe the young person's moral development and remorse; (4) document successful juvenile interventions that have been used for similar youth; and (5) describe how this young person's delinquent behavior could change if services met his/her needs.

> "The right to be heard would be, in many cases, of little avail if it did not comprehend the right to be heard by counsel."
> Powell v. Alabama, 287 U.S. 45, 68–69 (1932)

ADJUDICATION

My lawyer's telling me to plead guilty because the cop is going to get up on the stand and lie on me. I don't think that's right. I didn't sell anybody drugs. I was just hanging out.
—Andrew M., 15-year-old charged with distribution of cocaine

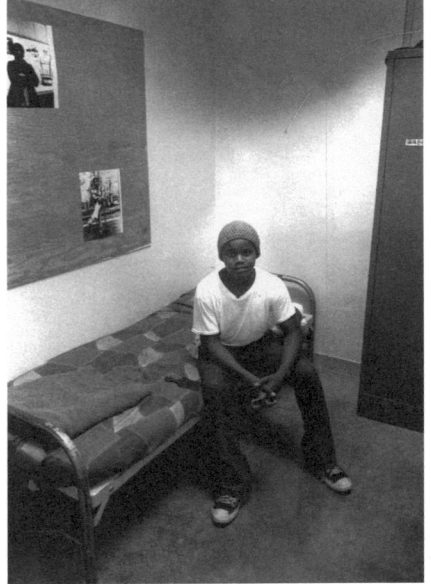

Juvenile adjudication hearings are the equivalent of trials in the adult criminal justice system. Prosecutors must prove "beyond a reasonable doubt" that youths committed the offenses charged. Juveniles do not have a constitutional right to trial by jury,[79] and consequently in most jurisdictions trials are held before judges. Many defense attorneys feel that it is more difficult to get an acquittal from a judge than a jury. It is therefore critical that counsel investigate cases thoroughly, utilize experts and other necessary resources at trial, and emphasize the heavy burden that the prosecution bears to prove guilt.

Sometimes, even if trials are not won, defenders can accomplish other goals. For example, they may present mitigating factors or other evidence that illustrates the limited role of their clients in the events at issue. That information can affect judges' decisions regarding dispositions.

The vast majority of juvenile cases result in plea bargains.[80] Counsel must ensure that clients understand the significance of the plea and its implications for the future. Young people often feel particular pressure simply to get some resolution to the matter. Counsel must ensure that clients have a complete understanding of what it means to plead guilty, especially since following the plea, if they violate probation they are more vulnerable to incarceration, and if they are arrested again, they are more likely to be handled in the adult system than if they were found not guilty at trial.

At the plea, judges should ask youth questions covering their mental capacity, whether the plea is voluntary, whether they understand the constitutional rights that are forfeited, and whether the admission has a factual foundation. In practice, however, guilty plea "colloquies" range in scope from extensive inquiries to a few very brief questions. Even under the best circumstances, young people have difficulty understanding what is going on. The IJA/ABA Juvenile Justice Standards state that juvenile courts should not accept pleas without determining that youth have the mental capacity to understand their legal rights and the significance of their pleas.[81]

With caseload pressures on courts and counsel, there is a real danger that the details of the adjudication process get swept away and that young people are lost in the confusion. In busy courtrooms, attorneys may describe plea offers in brief conversations with their clients. Counsel must take the time with their clients to fully explore the pleas, and alternatives to the pleas, in private areas where clients have opportunities to ask questions and express their concerns.

DISPOSITION

My lawyer doesn't know nothing about me, or what I do. She only met me twice for a few minutes and never returned my phone calls. She just started saying stuff to the judge about what I needed. What I needed was a new lawyer.
—*Jamie G., 16-year-old convicted of assault and larceny*

The dispositional phase of juvenile proceedings is the primary feature that distinguishes the juvenile system from adult criminal court. The purpose of the dispositional process is to develop plans for juveniles that meet their educational, emotional and physical needs, while protecting the public from future offenses. Typically, probation officers prepare reports to the court that state the circumstances of offenses, discuss youths' social and educational histories, review previous adjudications, and present other relevant information. Probation officers usually interview the juveniles and, if possible, their family members, teachers, and others who know them. Attitude may be a critical factor in the interviews: clients who appear cooperative, concerned, remorseful, and responsible will fare much better than those who do not. Sometimes courts order, or can be asked to order, assessments of young people, such as psychiatric, psychological, educational or neurological evaluations. These evaluations will be much more useful if counsel call or write the evaluator in advance to ask him or her to identify specifically the young person's emotional, educational and other needs and to request additional information to individualize dispositional planning.[82] Counsel must be sure that clients understand the process, are not frightened, and are encouraged to cooperate.

The dispositional phase of juvenile proceedings is the primary feature that distinguishes the juvenile system from adult criminal court.

Courts usually have very broad discretion in ordering dispositions. From less restrictive to more restrictive, potential dispositions include fines, restitution, community service, unsupervised probation while living at home, closely supervised probation at home, placement in a group home in the community, placement in a highly structured community residential program, placement in a "staff secure" (but not locked) program, and commitment to a locked institution. All of these dispositions, however, may not be available in every jurisdiction.

The IJA/ABA Juvenile Justice Standards provide that courts should order the least restrictive dispositions that satisfy the needs of both youth and society.[83] The Standards further provide that courts should also consider the individual needs and desires of youth in determining appropriate dispositions.[84]

In some jurisdictions, however, there are practical problems and due process concerns associated with the power of the administrative agency to control the specific placements of juveniles. Sometimes, the dispositional authority of the Court is limited. Crucial placement decisions are made by the agencies and the juvenile has little recourse.

At disposition hearings, counsel should call witnesses, such as family members, teachers, or ministers, and should present other evidence, such as letters of support, education or medical records, or evidence of participation in community or church activities. Counsel should be prepared to discuss the specific individual needs of their client, what services would meet those needs, what placements would not meet those needs and whether those needs can be met by the disposition proposed by probation. Answering the following questions, among others, may assist in identifying needs:

- Is the young person's misbehavior primarily a method of getting attention, gaining control or expressing anger?
- Does the young person need to improve his/her ability to express what he/she wants in effective, non-aggressive ways?
- Who are the individuals the young person is most attached to and what do they need to help the young person feel more competent or valued?
- Does the young person need to overcome a victim mentality?
- Does the young person need to learn how to feel more empathy for others?
- Does the young person have a substance abuse problem?
- At what grade level is the young person reading and is there a need to raise this reading level?
- At what grade level is the young person doing math and is there a need to raise this math level?
- Does the young person need to strengthen compensatory skills due to learning difficulties?
- What specifically is the source of disruptive school behavior?
- What specifically is the reason for school non-attendance?
- Does the young person have special interests that need to be built on by coaches, teachers and others through specific activities?
- What does the young person need to build on vocational interests?

- What do family members need to support the young person's school and job success?
- Is the young person in good health?

More than at any other stage of the juvenile justice system, counsel should explore every possible resource during the dispositional process. The process offers many opportunities to influence the outcome of their clients' cases. The lasting impact that dispositions may have on children's lives should not be underestimated. Clients who are incarcerated may have the course of their lives permanently altered, and it is crucial that attorneys dedicate every effort to favorable dispositions.

POST-DISPOSITIONAL REPRESENTATION

I know that I have clients that I should visit at the institution to find out what is going on before their review. But I have so many new clients that I am trying to keep from getting locked up in the first place. I don't have time to do everything and don't know what to do first.
— *Juvenile defense attorney*

Representation does not end at the dispositional hearing. There are many things that can be done for clients after the dispositional hearing: direct appeals of issues arising during the pretrial process or adjudication hearings, periodic reviews of dispositions, collateral reviews of adjudications, need for particular services such as drug or mental health treatment, or challenges to dangerous or unlawful conditions of confinement. The IJA/ABA Juvenile Justice Standards recognize the responsibility of counsel to continue representation in appropriate circumstances:

> The attorney should be prepared to counsel and render or assist in securing appropriate legal services for the client in matters arising from the original proceeding.[85]

Moreover, the Standards provide that lawyers who represent juveniles at trial or on appeal ordinarily should be prepared to assist clients in post-disposition actions either to challenge the proceedings leading to placements or to challenge the appropriateness of treatment facilities.[86] "Legal representation should also be provided the juvenile in all proceedings arising from or related to a delinquency or in need of supervision action, . . . including . . . other administrative proceedings related to the treatment process which may substantially affect the juvenile's custody, status or course of treatment. . ."[87]

The Standards provide that counsel should file appropriate notices of appeal and provide or arrange for representation perfecting appeals.[88] Technically, youth in juvenile court have the same appellate rights as their adult counterparts. As a practical matter, however, appeals in juvenile cases are rarely taken. Many defender offices, public and private, are not organized to take appeals: high caseloads prevent trial attorneys who know the record from pursuing appeals, and many offices cannot designate particular attorneys to work solely on appeals. Moreover, appellate work in juvenile cases is rarely cost-effective for appointed counsel. In addition, in many cases institutional commitments are relatively short, compared to adult prison sentences, which limits the time to perfect appeals. Finally, appellate courts are unlikely to allow juveniles to remain free while appeals are pending.

Despite these barriers, there are strong arguments to pursue appeals in appropriate cases. Felony adjudications (especially for such crimes as sex offenses), may have important implications for plea bargaining or sentencing if the youth gets in trouble in the future, either in juvenile court or adult criminal court. In addition, as states move to longer terms of commitment, there is more time to perfect appeals, and there are also more compelling reasons to challenge adjudications and dispositions.

Many states provide for periodic review of dispositions. Although in practice this is often a brief and perfunctory proceeding, it need not be. If there are grounds for release from confinement, or clients are not receiving needed services such as drug treatment or special education, or clients are in jeopardy due to lack of security or other dangerous conditions in institutions, or if home conditions have changed or community programs have openings, counsel can use dispositional reviews as opportunities to bring such matters to the attention of juvenile court judges.

In some jurisdictions, extraordinary writs such as *habeas corpus* and *mandamus* are available to challenge confinement as illegal, either because the confinement itself is unlawful (when minors, for example, are held in adult jail despite statutory prohibitions) or because juveniles have been held beyond the time permitted by statute or the conditions of confinement are harmful.

Youth may need particular services following dispositional hearings for a variety of reasons. Some dispositions make release from confinement contingent upon completion of specific programs in institutions. Thus, judges may require youth who have abused alcohol or illegal drugs to complete detoxification, treatment, and counseling before being released. In overcrowded state institutions, however, treatment programs are often over-subscribed and youth must wait until there are openings. Sometimes the delays in receiving treatment prevent youth from being released by the time set in dispositional orders. Such circumstances require vigorous advocacy by counsel.

In other situations, the nature of offenses, probation officers' reports, or independent evaluations prepared by the defense may reveal individual needs—such as emotional disturbance or suicidal behavior—that require particular treatment services during confinement. In addition, some youth need representation in related non-delinquency

Many states provide for periodic review of dispositions. Although in practice this is often a brief and perfunctory proceeding, it need not be.

proceedings, such as school suspensions, or proceedings to provide special education services while in placement.

For more than 25 years, federal civil rights litigation has revealed dangerous and unlawful conditions of confinement for young people detained in jails and local detention facilities or committed to state correctional institutions.[89] The litigation has been brought under the U.S. Constitution and state constitutions, as well as federal and state statutes. It has produced a body of case law that protects youth from harmful conditions and practices, and guarantees them certain necessary services.[90] Thus, youth have the right to protection from violent inmates,[91] abusive staff,[92] unsanitary living quarters,[93] excessive isolation,[94] and unreasonable restraints.[95] Youth are also entitled to adequate medical and mental health care;[96] access to counsel[97] and to family;[98] education, including special education for youth with disabilities;[99] and recreation, exercise, and other programming.[100]

When youth are held under dangerous or unlawful conditions, counsel may argue for release from the institution, special protection for clients or the provision of specific needed services within the institution. The IJA/ABA Standards recognize the importance of having counsel monitor conditions of confinement. The Standards state that legal representation should include litigation regarding the appropriateness of treatment provided under an original commitment order, the right to treatment, the non-statutory basis for reviewing the treatment provided, and, perhaps most importantly, conditions of confinement violative of the due process clause.[101]

Such representation can be provided in a variety of ways. In larger public defender offices, there are special litigation units that focus on "law reform" issues such as conditions of confinement. In other situations, public or private defenders can develop links with attorneys who can represent youth in conditions litigation. The attorneys can be in private law firms, undertaking such representation *pro bono publico*, or in public interest law offices that specialize in such litigation. In cooperative arrangements, the defenders can provide access to clients and initial information about the institutions, and the private attorneys can conduct the actual litigation.

CHAPTER 3

ASSESSMENT RESULTS

INTRODUCTION

This chapter sets forth the findings of the national assessment of lawyers defending children in juvenile court. The purpose of the survey was to understand the dimensions of the problems surrounding the availability of counsel and the quality of representation in juvenile delinquency proceedings. To our knowledge, this is the most comprehensive and extensive study of juvenile indigent defense services ever undertaken. Data collection and information-gathering included a national mail survey of juvenile defense attorneys, extensive on-site observations and interviews, and additional meetings with scores of public and private defenders, judges, child advocates, prosecutors, bar association officials, and policymakers.

In 1993, the American Bar Association released a report which suggested that there is a crisis in the area of indigent defense.[102] The "long-term neglect and underfunding" of indigent defense generally is exacerbated in the juvenile court setting, which has always competed for attention, status and resources with its adult counterparts. With increasingly severe consequences for delinquent behavior, crushing caseloads, more complicated procedural rules, shrinking public coffers, and already limited resources, it seemed urgent to generate additional information and insight into the needs and problems faced by juvenile defense attorneys.

In the course of our study, we observed many attorneys who vigorously and enthusiastically represented their young clients. Those lawyers challenged the prosecution to prove its case through pertinent evidentiary objections, motions, arguments, and contested hearings. In court, they were articulate and prepared. Their arguments were supported with relevant facts and law. When their clients were faced with lengthy incarceration, they often provided the court with compelling alternatives. The children they represented appeared to understand the proceedings. There was ongoing communication between children and their attorneys, both in and out of court. Those attorneys made good use of family members, other significant adults, experts, and potential service providers to demonstrate to the court the appropriateness of non-institutional placements.

But this type of vigorous representation was not widespread, or even very common. Often what we were told in interviews and what was reported in mail survey responses did not square with what we observed in courtrooms and detention centers. Assessment results raised serious concerns that the interests of many young people in juvenile

The "long-term neglect and underfunding" of indigent defense generally is exacerbated in the juvenile court setting, which has always competed for attention, status and resources with its adult counterparts.

court are significantly compromised, and that many children may literally be left defenseless.

Our intent is not to blame the many dedicated attorneys who are handling difficult cases and laboring under tremendous systemic burdens. Rather, we want to highlight their problems and needs in order to build their capacity and support their ability to provide improved legal services to children and youth.

The following discussion blends information obtained through the mail surveys, site visits, and additional meetings and focus groups.

GENERAL CHARACTERISTICS OF OFFICES AND PROGRAMS SURVEYED

Public Defender Offices

The public defender offices surveyed are mostly government agencies (83%), although a small portion are non-profit programs that provide representation under contract with the court or another government agency. In 76% of the jurisdictions, the chief public defender is appointed, rather than elected. The offices surveyed serve a range of jurisdictions from rural communities to major metropolitan areas. The salary figures reflect a very wide disparity among offices both for starting salaries and maximum salaries. Starting salaries were reported as low as $15,000 and as high as $73,000 with a mean salary just under $33,000. The maximum salary varied even more widely, with a low of $22,000 to a high of over $100,000. The mean maximum salary reported was $68,425. The level of financial compensation of public defenders is highly inconsistent across the country.

More than half of the public defender offices surveyed have at least some attorneys working exclusively on juvenile cases. In most of the offices, public defenders rotate from other courts to juvenile court, with the option of continuing to work there. In other offices, attorneys must rotate to adult criminal court in order to be promoted. Many public defenders do not stay in juvenile court very long. Among survey respondents, 55% stay less than 24 months.

Public defenders carry enormous caseloads. While caseloads varied, the average caseload carried by a public defender often exceeds 500 cases per year, and of that number, greater than 300 are juvenile cases.

Appointed Counsel

Nearly half of the appointed lawyers handling delinquency cases were solo practitioners. Of the remainder, most were in small firms and a handful were in medium or large-sized firms. Over half received appointment by a contract or by membership on a defender panel.

Appointed counsel had a wide range of experience. Their careers as lawyers ranged from less than two years to more than twenty years, and their years in juvenile court practice varied from less than one year to more than five years. They also have varied caseloads: a significant number carry under 50 cases, but about a fifth carry more than 200 cases. Most of the attorneys handle only a small proportion of juvenile cases. Only about a third handled more than 75 juvenile delinquency cases during the year preceding the survey.

Law School Clinical Programs

Since law school clinical programs handle delinquency cases primarily for their pedagogical value, they have very low caseloads. Of the programs responding to the survey, almost 75% include up to twenty students for two semesters. The caseloads of clinic students are generally very small, and are evenly divided between misdemeanors and felonies. Half of the clinical programs surveyed handle only delinquency cases, and the other half provide representation in delinquency cases as well as in other areas of the law.

Children's Law Centers

Children's law centers are typically private, non-profit, public interest law offices offering a range of services in several areas of the law that affect children. They usually receive financial support from charitable foundations, government grants, contracts for representation, state funds derived from interest on lawyers' trust accounts, and private contributions.

The two dozen children's law centers surveyed conduct a variety of work in the juvenile justice area. Almost 70% have between 1–5 full-time lawyers, but do not work exclusively on juvenile justice issues. Sixty-three percent of those surveyed represent individual children in delin-

> *"We do not consider whether, on the merits, Kent should have been transferred; but there is no place in our system of law for reaching a result of such tremendous consequences without ceremony—without hearing, without effective assistance of counsel, without a statement of reasons. It is inconceivable that a court of justice dealing with adults, with respect to a similar issue, would proceed in this manner."*
>
> *Kent v. United States, 383 U.S. 541, 554 (1966)*

quency cases. In addition, the children's law centers provide training, consultation and back-up for individual lawyers, class-action litigation, advocacy, and written materials including manuals, newsletters, articles, books, and other publications.

WAIVER OF COUNSEL

I've worked in rural counties where kids are being committed to institutions without so much as a petition being filed! How do I begin to live up to my obligations to my clients under circumstances like that? If the court doesn't value the appointment of counsel, how do you expect the clients to?

—Rural defender handling juvenile cases

One of the most disturbing findings of the survey is that large numbers of youth across the country appear in juvenile court without lawyers. This is so, despite the clear holdings of Kent v. United States[103] and Gault[104] that juveniles are constitutionally entitled to the assistance of appointed counsel at critical stages of delinquency proceedings. In survey and site visit jurisdictions around the country, project staff asked the reason for the failure to provide counsel to juveniles. One common justification was that children "waived" their right to counsel.

Such waiver of counsel by children has been strongly criticized as fundamentally unfair for several reasons.[105] As a result of immaturity or anxiety, unrepresented youth may feel pressure to resolve their cases and may precipitously enter admissions without obtaining advice from counsel about possible defenses or mitigation. Youth without counsel may be influenced by prosecutors or judges who must move their court calendars expeditiously. Youth may not understand the possible consequences of admitting offenses, such as potential incarceration and the resulting criminal records. Even where there is a colloquy with or before the judge, youth reported that they did not understand the terminology used or the principles discussed, or that they were intimidated by the proceedings and could not listen closely. Indeed, research and experience indicate that even adult defendants have difficulty understanding the courts' admonitions when they enter pleas, and there is no reason to believe that juveniles have any better understanding of the process.

Thirty-four percent of the public defender offices surveyed reported that some percentage of youth in the juvenile courts in which they work waive their right to counsel at the detention hearing: twenty-one percent say it happens 1–10% of the time, 5% say it happens 11–25% of the time, 4% say it occurs in 26–50% of the cases, and 4% say it happens 51–80% of the time. Reports by appointed counsel are very similar.

Of those juveniles who waive counsel, the waiver occurs after a colloquy in the presence of the judge slightly more than half the time (54%), but 46% of the public defenders say there is a colloquy only "some-

> *"Juvenile waiver of constitutional rights obviously must be more carefully proscribed than adult waiver because of the unrebuttable presumption, long memorialized by courts and legislatures, that juveniles lack the capacity to make legally binding decisions."*
>
> *J.M. v. Taylor, 276 S.E.2d 199, 203 (1981)*

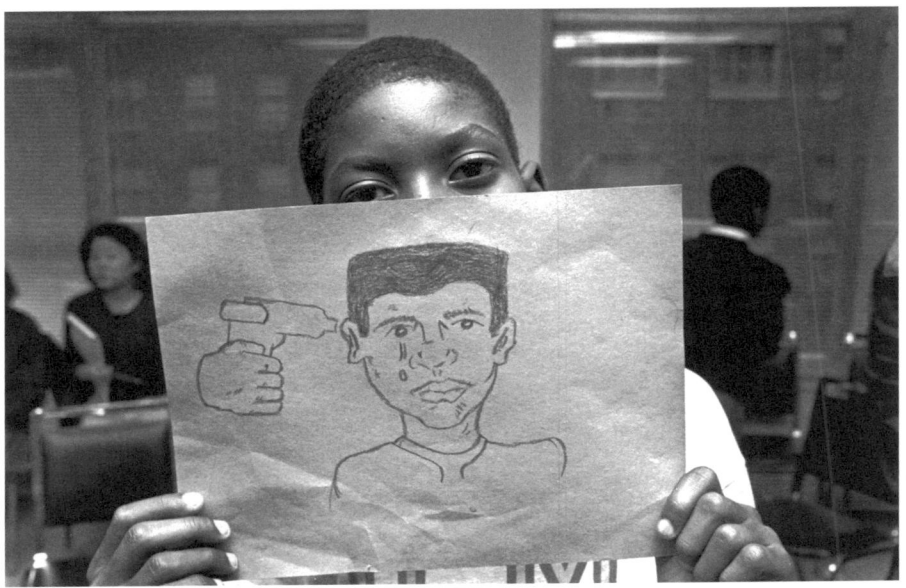

times" or "rarely." In addition, 45% of public defenders say the colloquy is only "sometimes" or "rarely" as thorough as the colloquy given to adult defendants. Although parents are present in court in the majority of cases where juveniles waive counsel, 12% of the public defenders said parents were only present "sometimes" and 10% said "rarely." Again, the reports by appointed counsel were very similar.[106]

Project staff learned that waivers of counsel are sometimes induced by suggestions that lawyers are not needed because no serious dispositional consequences are anticipated. Thus, judges and attorneys at one site reported that children in "lightweight" cases are "allowed" to waive counsel. Yet parents may be unable to provide helpful advice under such circumstances. In some situations, parents' views may actually conflict with those of their children. Indeed, it is clear that some parents pressure their children to waive counsel because they fear that they will have to pay for any counsel that is provided, or believe that complying with implied messages to waive counsel from judges will somehow lessen the blow for their children. Moreover, in a significant number of cases, parents are not present. These circumstances raise the possibility—perhaps the likelihood—that a substantial number of juvenile waivers are not "knowing and intelligent."

In other jurisdictions, the failure to provide children with counsel at critical stages of the proceedings may be the result of systemic triage decisions. Overburdened lawyers with high caseloads and limited resources have difficult decisions to make. They often have to give priority to more serious and complex cases, leaving others literally to fend for themselves. In rural areas, where pressure from the legal community to appoint lawyers is virtually nonexistent, youth waive counsel frequently. Furthermore, attorneys often have to travel hundreds of miles in rural counties to reach their clients, and these long distances inherently limit clients' access to counsel.

IMPACT OF CASELOAD LEVELS ON ACCESS TO COUNSEL AND QUALITY OF REPRESENTATION

Appointed counsel are the "McDonald's" of the industry, and the public defenders office is the 'M*A*S*H' unit. It's all triage no matter how you look at it.
   —*Supervising attorney, juvenile unit, public defender office*

Lawyers reported in the surveys and in on-site interviews that high caseloads were the single most important barrier to effective representation.

For children who are represented by counsel, lawyers reported in the surveys and in on-site interviews that high caseloads were the single most important barrier to effective representation. High caseload impacts on many aspects of representation. Attorneys with heavy caseload burdens find it difficult to meet with young clients and explain the proceedings before they appear at their detention hearings, conduct thorough investigations of the circumstances of the alleged offenses, learn about youths' ties to their families and to their communities, research and write individualized pretrial motions, keep informed on community-based alternatives to secure detention, develop dispositional plans that may be preferable to institutional confinement, follow up with clients during dispositional reviews, or monitor placement problems that may arise regarding needed services or conditions of confinement.

Most of the public defender offices surveyed (94%) have no cap on the number of juvenile cases they may handle. The great majority of attorneys feel that caseload pressures limit their ability to represent juvenile clients effectively: thirty-three percent say caseload pressures limit their ability "severely" or "considerably," another 39% say they "somewhat" limit their ability to provide representation. More than a third of those responding said that the time available to meet with and prepare clients before their cases are called is inadequate. In addition, almost half say that the time they have to confer with clients *after* their case is called in court is inadequate.

Appointed counsel reported fewer such problems. With much greater control over their caseload, few appointed counsel reported feeling that their ability to represent young clients effectively is limited by the size of their caseload. However, for appointed counsel carrying 200 or more cases, the impact on representation was similar to that experienced by public defenders with similarly high caseloads.

Site visits revealed the impact of high caseloads in more detail. At many of the sites, it was evident that—as a result of crushing caseloads and inadequate meeting space—lawyers often do not have the opportunity to interview clients adequately prior to detention hearings. At several sites, children literally met their lawyers as they sat down at counsel table in the detention hearing. Many youth were obviously confused, not knowing which one of the many adults in the courtroom was their lawyer. At other sites, it was common practice for attorneys to receive multiple case files only moments before representing those youth in court.

Space for interviewing was also a problem at several sites. When they *are* able to interview clients before detention hearings, defenders often have to conduct the interviews in group holding cells, where it is impossible to have confidential attorney-client communications. When rooms are set aside for interviews, they are often shabby and inadequate. One defender described the attorney interview rooms as "dark broom closets."

Counsel in such situations rely heavily on the information provided by probation or the prosecutor; such information is often incomplete or biased in favor of detention. There is no time to investigate the charges or to obtain information from social service agencies, schools, or families. There is no time for attorneys to develop relationships with clients or families. During detention hearings in court, there is no time to receive even the most basic facts from clients, let alone develop information that would be persuasive in arguing for dismissal, diversion, or release from custody. Caseload problems appear to be most pronounced before detention hearings. One attorney called the time available "pitifully insufficient."

Caseload affects representation in other ways as well. At several sites, probation officers reported that juveniles do not know who their lawyers are or what the charges are. This is so, probation officers said, at least 75% of the time. A public defender who carried as many as 200 active cases regretted that she is so "swamped" that it is hard to even explain "what's going on" to her clients.

Courtroom observations and discussions with attorneys, judges, and probation officers confirmed that the sheer number of cases in the system often result in bad outcomes for clients. Several lawyers told project staff that caseload pressures cause them to "plead out" cases rather than taking them to trial. Other attorneys admitted that caseload has a significant effect on their decision to file motions and fully investigate their cases.

The impact of all this on youth in juvenile court is devastating. Children represented by overworked attorneys receive the clear impression that their attorneys do not care about them and are not going to make efforts on their behalf. In one jurisdiction where it was clear that many attorneys had no relationship with their clients and demonstrated little involvement in the proceedings, a youngster said that his hearing "went like a conveyor belt." Lawyers operating under such pressures fail to offer meritorious arguments on behalf of their clients, and fail to present their clients in the best possible light. Furthermore, young people become passive and distrusting of their lawyers, sometimes withholding important information because, as one youngster put it, "it don't make no difference anyhow."

The impact of high caseloads has a debilitating impact on the attorneys as well. Burnout is a real problem for many caring juvenile defense attorneys. During one site visit, a veteran defense attorney wondered what would happen if caseloads were lowered: "I'm not sure that I could recapture the energy I once had to take more time

"There have been, at one and the same time, both an appreciation for the juvenile court judge who is devoted, sympathetic, and conscientious, and a disturbed concern about the judge who is untrained and less than fully imbued with an understanding approach to the complex problems of childhood and adolescence. There has been praise for the system and its purposes, and there has been alarm over its defects."
McKeiver v. Pennsylvania,
403 U.S. 528, 534 (1976)

with my cases, even if that time suddenly became available." More than one public defender felt hopeless about receiving any support from the public defender's office, noting that complaints about caseload are viewed as an inability of individual lawyers to handle their work—not as a systemic problem. Many lawyers expressed frustration at not being able to do all they wanted for their clients, and at the resulting unfairness to the children.

At the crucial first appearances in court, if judges ask about the events surrounding alleged offenses, the circumstances of arrests, the roles of other youth involved, or clients' prior contacts with the juvenile justice system, and attorneys do not have answers, the initial opportunity to present clients' cases in a favorable light is lost. Judges are left to review the uncontradicted allegations in the petitions. Based on those incomplete reviews, judges make early determinations regarding detention that may influence cases all the way until their dispositions.

Children represented by overworked attorneys receive the clear impression that their attorneys do not care about them and are not going to make efforts on their behalf.

Similarly, without meeting clients before court, or having adequate time to converse, there is no opportunity for counsel to develop information about families (immediate and extended), school, work, church, friends, or any other involvement by clients with their communities. Consequently, there are no foundations for informal dialogues with prosecutors or probation officers, or for formal arguments to the court, about the strengths of clients' families, the length and depth of ties to their communities, available role models, other sources of support or supervision, circumstances and resolutions of any prior contacts with the juvenile justice system, the likelihood that clients will run away or commit offenses before their next hearings, and, ultimately, the appropriateness of home detention, electronic monitoring, community programs, or other alternatives to secure detention.

The problems may be compounded during the later stages of pre-trial proceedings, adjudication, disposition, and post-disposition review. Ultimately, the result is likely to be a denial of the fundamental fairness that is at the core of due process of law.

APPOINTMENT OF COUNSEL

I try to develop a good rapport with my clients early on. I know that their initial impression of me makes a big difference as to how they will relate to me in the future.
—*Court appointed lawyer handling juvenile cases*

Among public defenders surveyed, 22% were first appointed at the intake hearing, and 56% at the detention hearing. Among private attorneys, 25% were assigned at the intake hearing, while 36% were appointed at the detention hearing. Forty-nine percent of public defenders report first meeting their clients before the detention hearing, as do 56% of private attorneys. However, data on the early appointment of counsel may be misleading. In many sites, a single attorney handles most detention hearings and accepts the appointment of counsel for a panel of attorneys, then cases are sent "downtown" for proper assignment of counsel later on. This means that children often do not have their own attorneys at initial court hearings or for a number of days afterward. This delayed assignment of attorneys has a significant impact on the investigation and development of cases and the formation of solid attorney-client relationships.

Although a paralegal or social worker could interview clients before the detention hearing, that is not common: only 25% of the public defenders said this happens "very often" or "often," and 58% said it occurs "rarely" or "never."

The site visits revealed that even when counsel was appointed early in the proceedings, attorneys were often unprepared for the detention hearing because they still did not have adequate time to interview their clients properly before the hearing began, nor did they have support staff who could conduct the interview on their behalf.

It is heartening that 78% of the public defenders were appointed at either the intake or detention hearing, but disappointing that 22% were appointed *after* the detention hearing, when courts had already made decisions about secure detention and, in many cases, youth had already entered admissions. It is also very troubling that more than half of the public defenders did not meet their clients before the detention hearing, and that almost half of the other appointed lawyers—who generally do not have the same caseload pressures as public defenders—did not meet their clients before the detention hearing.

At one site, staff watched an afternoon of detention hearings in which 29 cases were on the docket. The "defense" of these hearings was handled by an unsupervised law student who met the children in court for the first time; there was no background investigation or interview of children prior to court. No arguments were made for release, even though a number of the charges were minor, and the presentation of even minimal background information about the children and their families might have tipped the balance toward release. When asked about the failure to provide attorneys at the critical detention stage, public defender staff replied that the judicial officer in that court would "never release most of these children anyway," so the office had decided to deploy their scarce resources elsewhere.

In one case, there was no court translator, so a relative present in the courtroom was asked to translate for the non-English speaking juvenile. However, in the middle of the hearing, the judicial officer told the man he didn't have to translate "that part." In another case, the child's parent had not completely filled out the application for indigent public defender services and, rather than continue the case for a short while, the court held the case over until the next day, leaving the child in custody. These occurrences went unchallenged.

PRETRIAL PREPARATION AND TRIAL PERFORMANCE

I don't keep up with case law because I don't need to. I don't go to trial very often.
—Juvenile defense attorney

Inquiries into pretrial motions practice and trial performance yielded important information about a number of barriers to effective representation. High caseloads again create problems at this stage of delinquency proceedings. Attorneys who barely have time to cover all of their cases on a particular day are not likely to have the time or energy to research and write effective pretrial motions. The inadequacy (or absence) of training is another serious problem, as is lack of professional supports such as specialized texts, computerized legal research, access to paralegals, availability of bilingual staff or translators, and adequate space for interviewing and meeting with clients. The site visits confirmed the survey findings regarding pretrial preparation and trial performance. Public defender and private attorneys seldom do all the investigation needed in their cases. Defenders were concerned that they had not built relationships of trust with their clients, and their clients were equally dissatisfied. Shortly before trial, youth often did not know what was happening in their cases, and, as stated earlier, sometimes did not even know who their lawyers were.

We sought information on pretrial preparation and trial performance in a number of ways. First, the survey asked the practitioners whether they felt they were doing an adequate job preparing cases for trial. While self-reporting has obvious drawbacks, we hypothesized that if a significant number of attorneys report that they feel inadequately prepared, there are grounds for real concern, and the actual number of ill-prepared attorneys is likely to be much higher.

Second, the survey asked about areas that provide more objective though indirect indicators of pretrial and trial preparation, i.e., the filing of pretrial motions and the availability of resources for preparing and conducting trials. Finally, project staff assessed pretrial preparation and trial performance during the site visits.

Among the public defenders surveyed, 18% felt their performance was inadequate, 51% felt they were doing an adequate job, and 30% felt their performance was very adequate. The true implications of these responses are difficult to assess, but it is a matter of concern that almost one-fifth of the public defenders believe they are not doing an adequate job.

Only 30% of the public defenders and appointed counsel regularly file pretrial motions. Seventy percent of the public defenders and private attorneys said they file pretrial motions "sometimes," "rarely" or "never." This may be due in large measure to the fact that in the vast majority of these cases, pleas are entered early. Of the attorneys who do file motions, many acknowledged that they rely primarily on "boiler plate" motions and standard form pleadings.

Researchers have found that juvenile attorneys make few evidentiary objections, few motions to suppress evidence on constitutional grounds, call few witnesses, engage in only perfunctory cross-examination, and make only minimal, if any, closing arguments.[107]

While attorneys cited time and caseload pressures as one reason they do not file motions or aggressively try cases, it was clear that courthouse culture may play a role as well. In one jurisdiction, it was reported that attorneys do not file motions in order to maintain a "friendly" atmosphere in the courthouse, which is more important to them than "looking like a genius" on the day of the trial. Others reported that only "out-of-town" lawyers file motions. Another lawyer reported that after 16 years of practice in juvenile court, she had "only filed a few motions and could count my trials on one hand." A judge and a prosecutor reported that one of their only criticisms of attorneys was "when they took an adversarial role." Furthermore, not only would it be time-consuming for a defender with a large caseload to prepare even a few more juvenile trials each year, but if all the lawyers representing juveniles did so, it would put tremendous stress on courthouse calendars that rely significantly on negotiated pleas.

DISPOSITION

We rarely have the time or the opportunity to know the child or his family well enough to know what type of services may be needed at disposition. It would be so helpful to have a social worker or case manager to assist me in preparing for the disposition. I always feel like I'm selling my clients short.
—*Court appointed lawyer handling juvenile cases*

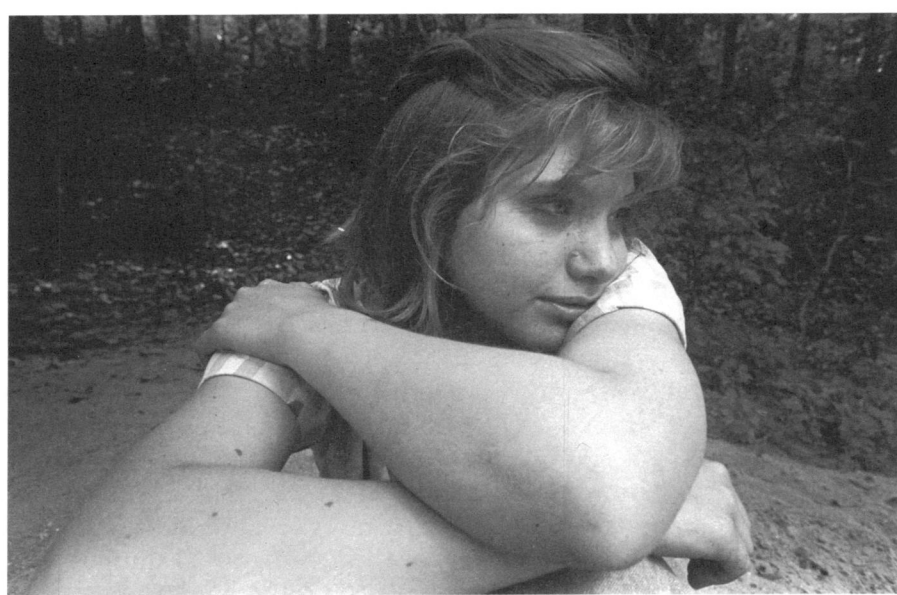

Attorneys were questioned about their perceptions of their own effectiveness at disposition, and about their access to social workers, case managers, dispositional advocates, and mental health experts who can evaluate the specific needs of clients and develop individualized disposition plans to present to the court.

Responding to the survey, most attorneys reported that they have adequate resources to prepare for disposition. At the site visits, however, a *very* different picture emerged: many attorneys openly acknowledged that their representation is deficient at the dispositional phase. The main reasons cited were the lack of time to keep up with placement options and other dispositional alternatives for the client; lack of time to prepare adequate dispositional plans; inability to work effectively with the administrative agencies that retain control of placements where the dispositional authority of the court is limited; and an overall lack of services for delinquents.

As at the other stages of representation, high caseloads make it difficult, if not impossible, for defenders to provide effective representation at dispositions. The problem is compounded by the lack of resources and support services. Although there was considerable variation among offices, many attorneys complained about inadequate access to experts who could conduct evaluations of clients or to paralegals or social workers who could do much of the work necessary to prepare dispositional plans.

Interviews with clients were very revealing and confirmed the shortcomings in dispositional representation. Many clients reported that they thought that their lawyers did not care about them. Some clients did not trust their attorneys and viewed them not as their advocates but as allies of the state. Some site visits revealed a factual foundation for the perception that a "cozy" relationship exists between some attorneys and juvenile court judges, particularly where the attorneys are dependent upon the court for appointments. A number of attorneys acknowledged that they "get along by going along." One frankly admitted that he considers the *judge* to be his client, and that he is not going to challenge the status quo or do anything that might upset his patron. The regular practice in one court, unchallenged by defense counsel, is to incarcerate children for failure to go to school as ordered. In another jurisdiction, children can be found "unruly" if they are involved in interracial relationships and parents report this activity to the court. Attorneys admitted that incarceration for truancy or unruliness seemed Draconian, but they opted for a pleasant courtroom experience by keeping in the court's good graces. This problem was particularly prevalent in rural areas.

These findings are of serious concern, particularly because dispositional hearings are often the last and most important opportunity for counsel to protect the interests of their clients. Although some attorneys provide excellent representation—with experts available to conduct client evaluations and social workers to prepare individualized dispositional plans—many attorneys are unable to provide judges with any alternatives to the recommendations of probation officers.

> *"Armed with adequate information, counsel can then present the court with all reasonable alternative dispositions to incarceration and should have taken the initial steps to secure the tentative acceptance of the child into those facilities."*
>
> D.D.H. v. Dostert,
> 269 S.E.2d 401, 412
> (1980)

Several researchers have emphasized the need for juvenile defense attorneys to independently explore dispositional alternatives, to seek expert advice to assure appropriate and individualized treatment for their clients, to utilize the support of volunteer advocates and other support personnel, and to take an active role in the dispositional hearing.[108] It has been reported that in some cases, children represented by retained counsel are more likely to receive such assistance, in large part because their families can afford to pay for it. Retained counsel sometimes spend more time with the child and family, are better prepared to cast a positive light on the child's character and behavior, and are often able to suggest specific alternative dispositions that parents are willing and able to pay for. As a result, the few children who can afford to retain counsel are sometimes more successful in convincing the judge either that court involvement is unnecessary or that some minimal intervention is appropriate.[109]

Children who do not have access to such defense services at disposition are at a significant disadvantage.[110] Thus, attorneys need to be knowledgeable about eligibility requirements and funding mechanisms for various programs, including special education; "nonlegal" topics such as the causes of delinquency and family conflict; policies and procedures of the agencies coming into contact with the court; ways to use the skills of other professionals such as psychiatrists or psychologists; and the availability of local programs and facilities for juvenile offenders.[111]

POST-DISPOSITIONAL REPRESENTATION

I recognize that the post-dispositional issues my clients face are compelling. But come on, how do you really expect me to keep up with those issues when I can barely manage my caseload day to day?
—*Public defender, juvenile division*

Almost one-third of public defenders and 41% of appointed counsel end their representation of juveniles at the disposition hearing. Defenders rarely take appeals in juvenile cases. Among public defender offices responding to the survey, 32% are not even authorized to handle appeals. Of the offices that do handle appeals, 46% took no appeals in juvenile cases during the year prior to the survey. Site visits confirmed these findings. One public defender reported that she handles her own appeals but must do so on nights and weekends because of the pressure of her "regular" caseload. The failure of some public defender offices to give any leeway in case assignments for lawyers taking appeals has operated as a disincentive and created hardships for those taking appeals.

Appointed lawyers also take appeals infrequently. Among the appointed lawyers surveyed, three-quarters were authorized to handle appeals but 79% took none during the prior year.

"The same concern for the seriousness of juvenile detention which requires the recognition that juveniles have constitutional rights to procedural protections at juvenile commitment hearings motivates this Court to recognize that incarcerated juveniles have a right of access to the courts comparable to incarcerated adults."
John L. v. Adams,
750 F.Supp. 288, 291
(M.D. Tenn. 1990)

As noted earlier, there are a number of reasons why appeals are so rare. Caseload pressures make it difficult for trial counsel to also handle appeals. In fact, in one site many lawyers candidly reported that vertical representation (i.e., the attorney who represented the youth in juvenile court handles the appeal) creates a disincentive to appeal. Other lawyers noted that the slow time frame for appeals makes them of limited use in juvenile cases. Indeed, in one site, most juveniles are not even regularly advised of their right to appeal.

In most juvenile cases, children who are made wards of the court will be under juvenile court jurisdiction for periods ranging from one to several years. That so many public defenders end their representation at the dispositional hearing means the children's original attorneys often do not provide continuing representation at subsequent dispositional reviews. In one jurisdiction, the public defenders, beset by staff shortages and heavy caseloads, lobbied for a change in the law so they would not be required to represent children in post-dispositional status. When asked about the impact this would have on continuity of representation, they reported that they did not view the role of the attorney at such hearings as particularly "useful" anyway.

Of those offices surveyed that do represent youth at dispositional reviews, three-fourths usually interview the youth before the hearing, but only slightly more than half usually review the treatment plans and interview probation or parole officers before the review hearing. Further, fewer than one-third of the respondents usually interview treatment staff, investigate alternative placements, or monitor implementation of treatment plans for juveniles in placement.

The appointed lawyers who continue to provide representation after the dispositional hearings generally appear to do more than public defenders. Virtually all appointed counsel interview the child before the review hearing; 85% interview probation or parole officers before the hearing; 72% review the treatment plan; about two-thirds interview the child's family; and the same percentage investigate alternative placements before the hearing. However, fewer than a quarter often monitor the implementation of their clients' treatment plans.

Almost half of the public defender offices report that they "rarely" (37%) or "never" (10%) handle extraordinary writs. Almost half (48%) handled no writs in the previous year, and another 41% handled ten or less.

Ninety percent of the public defender offices "never" or "rarely" file separate individual actions on behalf of juveniles, and 79% "never" or "rarely" represent juveniles in related non-delinquency proceedings such as school discipline or special education proceedings. Ninety percent of the private attorneys "rarely" or "never" commence separate proceedings for clients outside of the delinquency cases, and just over two-thirds "rarely" or "never" represent clients in related non-delinquency proceedings.

Ninety-one percent of the public defender offices do not engage in class action litigation on behalf of juveniles. However, a number of attorneys reported that they have referred clients to other counsel in relation to institutional conditions cases.

The failure to maintain representation during the entire period of juvenile court jurisdiction is a serious problem. It means that attorneys do not monitor their clients' progress in programs or institutional placements or assure that the services ordered by courts are actually provided and that conditions in programs and institutions are lawful. As a consequence, needed modifications in court orders may not come to official attention until youth have acted out or committed new offenses. New counsel appointed at the post-disposition stage are unlikely to develop a relationship with the children or their families, or have the background needed to best articulate their clients' needs and capabilities.

The failure to maintain representation during the entire period of juvenile court jurisdiction is a serious problem.

TRAINING AND SUPPORT SERVICES

Lack of training on effective representation of juveniles at all stages of the proceedings was cited as a contributor to inadequate representation at all the sites visited and surveyed. Only 38% of the appointed lawyers reported the availability of a criminal law training program for representing indigent juvenile defendants. Of the public defender offices, 78% do not have a budget for lawyers to attend training programs, 50% do not have a training program for all new attorneys, 48% do not have an ongoing training program, 46% do not have a section in the office training manual devoted to juvenile delinquency practice, 42% do not have a specialized manual for juvenile court lawyers, 35% do not include juvenile delinquency work in the general training program, 32% do not have any training manual, and 32% do not have a training unit.

When training is provided to juvenile defenders, there are significant gaps in the topics covered: seventy-four percent of the public defender offices do not cover pretrial motions practice, 65% do not cover transfer of juveniles to adult court, 60% do not cover client-specific dispositions, 58% do not cover detention alternatives, 54% do not cover child development and issues of capacity, and 50% do not cover how to show amenability to treatment in transfer hearings.

During site visits, juvenile defenders repeatedly stated that they need additional training on dispositional alternatives, funding mechanisms, and working with other systems such as special education. Several court personnel also noted the need for training on communication skills with children and families, multicultural sensitivity, and how to handle difficult ethical situations. Many also reported an interest in developing basic trial advocacy skills.

Despite this gap in most places, site visits revealed some very positive training programs, many of which could be emulated elsewhere. Some offices provided extensive training prior to assigning cases to lawyers; others had creative training mechanisms such as mentoring by experienced attorneys, brown bag lunches on current juvenile justice issues, or the provision of a yearly training "allowance" per attorney.

In addition to training gaps, juvenile defenders also lack support services. Among public defender offices, 42% of the offices do not have specialized texts on juvenile law, and 64% do not have access to Westlaw or Lexis. Appointed counsel have fewer resources: about half lack specialized texts on juvenile law and brief banks, and 60% do not have access to Westlaw or Lexis.

Although most public defender offices have "access" to investigators, 56% do not have paralegals. Among appointed counsel, 22% do not have access to investigators and 47% do not have paralegals. Moreover, site visits revealed that the procedures necessary to request investigators and paralegals were often so complex and time-consuming that lawyers simply opted for managing without them.

Attorneys at a number of sites voiced a need for staff social workers or case managers to assist in client needs assessment and alternative disposition plans.

Attorneys at a number of sites voiced a need for staff social workers or case managers to assist in client needs assessment and alternative disposition plans. Others spoke of the need for basic secretarial support, investigators, paralegals, and computers. Amazingly, at one site the lawyers did not even have the very basics of law practice - desks, telephones, files, or offices. They just used the bare counsel table in the courtroom to conduct their business. If their client wants to reach them by telephone, the client is given the number to the judge's chambers and the judge is supposed to pass the message on to the lawyer.

Half (51%) of the public defender offices do not have bilingual attorneys available to communicate directly with clients who speak the first most commonly spoken language other than English, and a quarter of the offices do not have any translators available for clients who speak the first most commonly spoken language other than English. Further, most public defender offices (83%) do not have bilingual attorneys available to communicate directly with clients who speak the second most commonly spoken language other than English, and 43% do not have any translators for clients who speak that language.

PRIORITIES FOR IMPROVING THE QUALITY OF REPRESENTATION

During the site visits, project staff asked attorneys and court personnel to define their greatest priorities for removing barriers and improving the quality of representation in their jurisdiction. The stated priorities varied somewhat, depending upon whether the respondent was a defense attorney, prosecutor, judge, or probation officer. However, certain themes emerged from all respondents.

Judges, in particular, voiced a need for more "help" from defense attorneys on dispositional issues. They specifically called for more background information on education and special education needs, medical and psychological work-ups, and family characteristics. There was agreement among all respondents that juvenile attorneys need to be better trained about dispositional programs in their jurisdictions, and the development of alternative disposition plans for special situations. Many mentioned the need for the system as a whole to develop an increased range of services as an important priority. The need for increased dispositional options for girls was viewed as a particular problem.

Several other training issues emerged. A number of respondents spoke of the need to improve attorneys' "interpersonal skills" in relating to children and parents, and their understanding of adolescent and child development. The need to improve multicultural sensitivity was also raised by a number of respondents. Similarly, one respondent felt that attorneys need to learn how to see and present the client as a "real person—with a life." A number of respondents suggested that such training could be offered by local law schools and clinics.

Some respondents felt that systemic management issues were the highest priority. These included assuring reasonable caseloads and sufficient time to meet with clients before court hearings. One respondent said that caseloads in her jurisdiction should be cut in half. Another mentioned the need to assure early appointment of counsel, so that contact with clients occurs as soon as possible. Respondents also mentioned the need for back end continuity of services—the need to monitor how children are actually doing in placement or other dispositional programs. Also, several respondents pointed to a need for improved support services, such as social workers or paralegals who can do background investigation for detention release hearings and help prepare plans for disposition hearings.

Systemic priorities for other respondents were more fundamental: assuring that all children have attorneys, and that funding issues do not determine whether children are represented.

Several comments focused on the status of juvenile attorneys. One judge suggested that public defender offices should put their best attorneys in juvenile court, and not just use juvenile court as a training ground. Other respondents focused on payment issues as they relate to status. One judicial officer felt strongly that attorneys should be paid by the hour for the work they actually do on each case, rather than on the typical artificial payment scale which reduces the incentive for lawyers to spend more out-of-court time with clients and their families.

CHAPTER 4

PROMISING APPROACHES TO EFFECTIVE REPRESENTATION

While the survey revealed substantial deficiencies in access to counsel and the quality of representation in juvenile court, it would be incorrect to conclude that effective representation of young people cannot and does not exist. Project staff observed many individual defenders around the country who were delivering first-rate legal services to their young clients. Defender programs that appear to be of high quality have the following characteristics in common:

- Limited caseloads;
- Support for entering the case early, and the flexibility to represent the client in related collateral matters (such as special education);
- Comprehensive initial and ongoing training and available resource materials;
- Adequate non-lawyer support and resources;
- Hands-on supervision of attorneys; and,
- A work environment that values and nurtures juvenile court practice.

As described throughout this report, the negative impact of caseload pressures at every stage of the delinquency process undermines effective representation. Some defender offices have attempted to address this problem internally, by allowing attorneys to ask for temporary relief from new case assignments if their caseloads are too burdensome.[113] Others have responded to post-dispositional caseload pressures by ensuring that incarcerated youth have the right of access to the courts,[114] or by forming linkages with state agencies and obtaining state funds to provide much needed post-commitment representation.[115] And others have established specialized units within the office to siphon off the time-consuming cases of habitual offenders or those cases pending transfer to adult court that require special attention and skill.[116]

Entering the case as early as possible, and having adequate time to meet with the client, their family, and others, enables counsel to provide much more effective representation at the detention hearing and throughout the case. It is the policy of some defender offices to enter the case shortly after the arrest; because the offices are located in the communities they serve, the lawyers are known to local residents who are encouraged to call immediately upon arrest or after being approached by the police.[117]

Recognizing the critical importance of training, some defender offices have stretched their budgets to establish high-quality, in-house training units that deliver comprehensive training to lawyers before their representation of children commences.[118] These programs are extensive, sometimes 5–8 weeks in duration, and incorporate many creative techniques such as role playing, moot court, interactive videos, combined with the more traditional format of lectures, seminars and even homework. Some training programs are open to appointed counsel and other lawyers in the community. In some jurisdictions, low-cost or free training is ongoing and offered throughout the year.

Since there is often an attenuated relationship between the adult and juvenile units within a public defender office, with the more experienced attorneys being located "downtown," the availability of adequate supervision for juvenile defenders is sometimes lacking. Recognizing good supervision as critical to effective representation, some public defender offices have developed ways to assure that juvenile defenders can access the expertise of their colleagues. In one office, each attorney who has been there less than three years is matched with a senior attorney, who serves as their mentor and confidant. The mentor is responsible for routinely meeting with the attorney, discussing pending cases in detail, observing and critiquing hearings and trials, and reviewing case files. Mentors supervise only one attorney at a time. The mentor/mentee pairs rotate every six months so as not to get "stale" or place too much of a burden on the mentor. The trial chief and assistant trial chiefs also provide additional supervision to the attorneys.[119] Other offices provide supervision by putting small groups of lawyers, with differing levels of experience, on teams. Each team of lawyers meets regularly to discuss each other's cases.[120]

The availability and adequacy of non-lawyer resources is also necessary for effective representation. In addition to support staff, other non-lawyer resources include investigators, paralegals, social workers, mental health experts, and interpreters. One way defenders have managed to get this support is through the mobilization of volunteer labor such as college, graduate and law students. With appropriate training, college students can serve as investigators or as tutors or mentors for delinquents; graduate students with social work or psychology backgrounds can assist with client evaluations and develop dispositional plans; and law students can assist with overall case preparation including interviewing, researching and writing motions and briefs, and responding to post-dispositional problems. Many programs have successfully utilized these resources at little or no cost.[121]

Some defender offices have found creative ways in which to respond to other compelling issues facing their clients, such as the disproportionate overrepresentation of children of color in juvenile detention facilities. For example, one public defender office obtained federal funds to initiate a project aimed at reducing the numbers of nonwhite youth confined at an already-overcrowded detention center. A lawyer/social worker team is stationed at the facility, and depending on the point at which they intervene in the case, they will bring the case back into court and vigorously advocate for alternatives to the institutional placement.[122] To address fragmented legal services, one defender office forged a formal partnership with a Legal Services office and obtained a grant to integrate criminal and civil representation of juvenile offenders.[123]

While the above discussion has focused on the resourcefulness of public defenders and other appointed counsel, examination of the role of law school clinical programs and non-profit children's law centers is also instructive. Law school clinical programs and children's law centers play a crucial part in building the capacity of the legal system to provide adequate representation to delinquent youth and establishing a future "corps of excellence" among juvenile defenders. Even though they handle only a small number of cases, their value in improving the practice of children's law is very important.

Law school clinical programs handling delinquency cases have a dual mission of representation and instruction. While serving as excellent pedagogical means for teaching students practical skills and substantive law, they also usually provide excellent representation for juvenile clients. These clinics generally handle very low caseloads so that they can effectively teach students as they work through a case.[124]

Law school clinics can serve as models for providing high quality representation. Because they can take the time on each case to conduct a thorough investigation, interview the client and the client's family, investigate alternatives to secure detention and institutional confinement, examine all potential legal issues, prepare for each hearing, and plan each disposition, they have a body of experience and a set of reg-

The availability and adequacy of non-lawyer resources is also necessary for effective representation.

Law school clinical programs and children's law centers play a crucial part in building the capacity of the legal system to provide adequate representation to delinquent youth and establishing a future "corps of excellence" among juvenile defenders.

ular procedures that can benefit public defenders and appointed counsel. New practitioners can learn the value (some might say the luxury) of complete representation by looking at law school clinics. In addition, when new statutes or court decisions make it possible to try novel arguments and bring unusual motions, law school clinics typically have the ability to conduct the legal research and preparation necessary for effective presentation to juvenile courts. Law school clinics can also serve as laboratories for new office structures, new resources, new technologies, and other new techniques to improve representation.

Moreover, law school clinics can be valuable assets to juvenile defenders in their communities. For example, law school clinical professors can assist defenders by furnishing written materials adapted from clinic materials, and teaching in training programs. Clinics can assist practitioners in taking appeals in juvenile cases, both in framing issues to raise on appeal and in writing appellate or *amicus* briefs. Some law school clinics become involved in important impact litigation cases, and students become invaluable investigators, researchers and partners in the case. Law school clinics are also a crucial source of well-trained, knowledgeable, and experienced law students for internships.

In addition, the last twenty years has seen a growth in the number of small non-profit children's law centers that work on a range of legal issues affecting children. Similar to law school clinics, children's law centers generally represent small numbers of young people in delinquency proceedings, and do not typically experience the caseload pressures of their public defender counterparts. Also like law school clinics, children's law centers can put substantial resources into each case: for example, they often have paralegals and social workers on staff who can work closely with clients and families while preparing the case. They can put the time into exploring the best alternatives to detention or incarceration. They can truly serve as models for complete, holistic legal representation.

The assessment revealed that over 80% of the children's law centers surveyed engage in advocacy; 83% provide consultation; 42% conduct class action litigation; 79% conduct training; and 50% prepare and disseminate publications. Several also reported specialized areas of practice that are closely related to delinquency proceedings, such as special education, school expulsions and mental health. Thus, children's law centers can provide important backup to public defenders and appointed counsel in critical areas.

Patricia Puritz

Recommendations and Implementation Strategies

CHAPTER FIVE

RECOMMENDATIONS AND IMPLEMENTATION STRATEGIES

The Juvenile Justice and Delinquency Prevention Act (1974), the National Advisory Committee for Juvenile Justice and Delinquency Prevention (1980), and the American Bar Association (1980) have set forth standards specifically requiring all juveniles to be represented at all phases of the delinquency process. While some juveniles receive high quality representation from public and private defenders, many do not have access to counsel or effective representation from arrest through disposition and post-disposition. Based on the assessment, this report calls for increased resources for juvenile defenders, improvement in the quality of representation at all stages of juvenile cases and continued collection of information about representation in juvenile court.

A. STATE AND LOCAL JURISDICTIONS SHOULD INCREASE THE RESOURCES AVAILABLE TO SUPPORT REPRESENTATION OF JUVENILES IN DELINQUENCY PROCEEDINGS.

1. Local jurisdictions should ensure that sufficient resources are available to increase the number of attorneys representing juveniles in delinquency proceedings and increase the availability of non-lawyers with special expertise to assist in case planning and representation.

Ensuring adequate numbers of attorneys would address the problems of excessively high caseloads and unavailability of lawyers at key stages of the delinquency proceedings, including detention hearings and appeals. Increasing the number of attorneys can be accomplished in a variety of ways: hiring additional public defenders, establishing contract defender offices, expanding appointed attorney panels, and collaborating with state and local bar associations, private law firms, and local law school clinics. Steps should also be taken to increase the availability of non-lawyer support from social workers, investigators and graduate students to help manage caseloads and improve the quality of representation.

2. Agencies responsible for funding defender programs should ensure that a fair and equitable share of available resources is allocated for juvenile representation.

Guideposts for measuring equity are comparability in funding between juvenile defenders and adult defenders, and between juvenile defenders and prosecutors. Juvenile defenders should also have comparable access to training, investigators, social workers, mental health professionals, interpreters, law libraries, appellate and other support services, and computer systems, files, secretarial support, paralegals and other office support.

3. Courts and others responsible for the allocation of defender funding should ensure that strategic decisions in juvenile cases are made on the basis of sound legal practice rather than funding incentives.

In some jurisdictions, lawyers do not receive an adequate salary or hourly rate or are not adequately compensated for motions or other proceedings necessary to properly protect the interests of the client. In other jurisdictions, lawyers are paid a flat fee, no matter how complex the case, which acts as a disincentive to provide vigorous defense. Courts and local bar associations should work together to establish a fair fee schedule or compensation system. The hourly rate, fee schedule or compensation available to juvenile defenders should be commensurate with that provided for comparable legal work in the community. Fee schedules should be flexible enough to allow for compensation for a broad range of legal work needed to fully represent a minor, including development of dispositional alternatives, work on related educational or mental health issues and post-dispositional review.

B. STATE AND LOCAL JURISDICTIONS SHOULD IMPROVE THE QUALITY OF REPRESENTATION OF JUVENILES IN DELINQUENCY PROCEEDINGS.

1. Attorneys representing minors in delinquency proceedings should receive comprehensive training.

Each lawyer who represents juveniles should receive training prior to representation in juvenile court and regularly thereafter. Trainers should use innovative and interactive techniques, including audiotapes, videotapes, mock hearings, or regional meetings with teleconferencing to ensure that trainings are flexible, affordable, effective and accessible to attorneys in distant areas. The curriculum for the trainings should be updated regularly and be comprehensive, including, at a minimum, child development, communicating with young clients, multicultural issues, knowledge of community resources, diversion, informal case resolution, ethics, transfer/waiver hearings, and related legal issues such as custody, education, mental health, and child welfare.

2. Every attorney's caseload should be low enough to permit the attorney to provide quality representation to juveniles in delinquency proceedings.

The number of cases handled by an attorney at any given time is the single most important factor in determining quality of representation.

Juvenile defenders and appointed counsel should have the discretion to decide whether or not to accept a case if, in their opinion, they cannot represent their client effectively due to an overwhelming caseload.

3. The legal profession should elevate the status of attorneys providing representation in juvenile court.

Defender offices should permit attorneys to specialize and remain in juvenile court practice. Promotion should not be conditioned upon rotation out of juvenile court. Attorneys in juvenile court should represent every experience level, and juvenile court should not be used simply as a training ground for new attorneys.

4. Courts, bar associations or agencies with authority to certify or appoint counsel should adopt minimum standards for representation in juvenile court.

Minimum standards of representation should address:

- Guarantees that every juvenile has counsel, that the right to counsel is not waived, and that the juvenile is represented from the earliest stages of the proceeding through post-disposition stages;
- Experience and qualifications of the attorney, including training and familiarity with relevant law and local practice;
- Expectations for actual representation, including interviewing clients thoroughly at every stage of the proceeding, sensitivity to multicultural issues, conducting adequate investigation, preparing the case and filing appropriate pretrial motions, ensuring that the child understands the proceedings and their outcome, exploring alternative dispositions, familiarizing oneself with local resources, pursuing appeals or other legal proceedings necessary to protect the child's interests, representing clients in post-disposition reviews, and monitoring implementation of the disposition; and,
- Systemic issues such as caseload limitation, adequate law libraries, private space to interview clients, adequate computer systems, files, secretarial support, and access to paralegals, social workers, interpreters and investigators.

C. STATE AND LOCAL JURISDICTIONS SHOULD COLLECT DATA ON THE REPRESENTATION OF JUVENILES IN DELINQUENCY PROCEEDINGS.

1. Local courts or bar associations should routinely collect data regarding representation of juveniles to identify systemic weaknesses, and provide a baseline for improvement.

The data collected should identify how many juveniles are represented or have waived counsel at each stage of the proceedings, including: arrest, detention, pretrial proceedings, transfer, adjudication and post-adjudication. The data collected should also identify attorney caseloads, court caseloads, and the caseloads of other professionals providing services to juveniles. Data on attorney salaries, forms of attorney compensation (flat fee or per hour basis), and cost-per-juvenile expenditures should also be tracked. Juvenile defenders should be regularly polled regarding what they need to improve the quality of representation offered to young people, and their recommendations should be presented to state and local bar associations, community groups, state legislatures and agencies, Congress, and the federal government.

2. Jurisdictions should conduct local workload assessments in order to determine the appropriate caseload and staffing needs for each jurisdiction.

In view of the critical importance of caseload at all stages of the delinquency process, it is necessary that jurisdictions conduct workload assessments in order to set caseloads at appropriate levels.

3. A statewide agency or organization should compare and publish local assessments.

Statewide assessments can pinpoint which jurisdictions provide high rates of representation, manage attorney and court caseloads well and otherwise act as possible models for other jurisdictions to follow. Comparing local expenditures can also identify inequities and problems in funding, especially attorney compensation. Publication of the results of this assessment will increase public awareness of juvenile justice issues, and allow other groups to participate in finding solutions.

The implementation of these recommendations to improve young people's access to counsel and quality of representation at all stages of the juvenile court process requires simultaneous action by many different groups. Some of those activities might include the following:

State Legislatures Should...

- Examine the extent to which children are appearing in court without lawyers.
- Conduct oversight hearings which focus on children's access to legal representation and quality of such representation.
- Gather regular information from judges, attorneys, bar representatives and citizens groups, on issues relating to the representation of children, especially in delinquency proceedings.
- Ensure that adequate funding is available to guarantee quality representation for children, including funds for training, non-lawyer support and resources, manageable caseloads, and adequate compensation.

- Ensure that the principles of due process are protected in juvenile court proceedings, especially when a child's deprivation of liberty is at stake.

State and Local Bar Associations Should...

- Establish a juvenile rights committee that annually assesses juvenile defender services.
- Assess optimal caseloads, appropriate compensation, training and other resources available for juvenile defenders.
- Assess comparability of resources available to juvenile defenders with those available to adult criminal defenders and prosecutors.
- Conduct ongoing training for juvenile law practitioners, building on the strengths of juvenile law clinics or juvenile law centers in the state.
- Encourage law firms and members of the private bar to include representation of juveniles in delinquency proceedings as part of their pro bono work.
- Work with state legislatures to advocate for improved juvenile defender services.
- Support and create activities that elevate the status of juvenile court practice.

Public Defender Offices Should...

- Ensure that attorneys have manageable caseloads.
- Ensure that juvenile defenders have the resources available to investigate and prepare cases properly from commencement through appeal, including access to needed social workers, investigators, experts and interpreters.
- Ensure that all juvenile defenders receive regular, ongoing and comprehensive training, and supervision from experienced juvenile defenders.
- Include appointed lawyers in training and other substantive law programs.
- Encourage attorneys to specialize in juvenile defender work and eliminate any promotional or other office policies that act as barriers to remaining in such work.
- Take steps to improve unacceptable and unlawful conditions in facilities where clients are confined.
- Stay involved in juvenile cases after disposition to ensure that juveniles receive appropriate post-dispositional legal services.
- Become familiar with local services and encourage the development of community-based services.

Law Schools Should...

- Encourage interest in juvenile justice issues through academic course offerings and clinical programs.
- Collaborate with other university cross-disciplinary programs (such as social work, education, psychology and medical schools) to develop internships and volunteer work with juveniles.

- Sponsor and coordinate continuing education and training programs with children's law centers, bar associations and others, to ensure that juvenile defenders receive comprehensive training.

Congress Should...

- Examine the extent to which exceedingly high caseloads cripple the juvenile indigent defense system.
- Examine the extent to which children are appearing in court without lawyers.
- Hold oversight hearings to document the quality and accessibility of lawyers in juvenile court and the protection of children's rights.
- Provide funding to establish a training academy for public defenders and other lawyers for juveniles that is equivalent to training available to juvenile court judges and prosecutors.

State Advisory Groups Should...

- Monitor and assess the accessibility and quality of juvenile defender services, using professional standards of representation.
- Use discretionary funding, challenge grants, and other resources to support enhanced defender services.
- Provide oversight on post-dispositional legal issues relating to unlawful conditions of confinement.
- Sponsor training on effective representation for public defenders and other court-appointed counsel.

Citizens Groups Should...

- Become familiar with the organizations or individuals representing children in their community.
- Request permission to attend juvenile court delinquency proceedings.
- Request permission to visit juvenile detention and correctional facilities.
- Visit community-based programs for juveniles.
- Invite experts in juvenile law to speak at meetings and social events.
- Develop contacts within the courts, bar associations and State Advisory Groups to facilitate ongoing communication.

Juvenile Courts Should...

- Ensure that no juvenile goes unrepresented at any critical stage of the juvenile court process.
- Ensure that counsel representing juveniles are appropriately trained and adequately compensated and that minimum standards are met.
- Collect data on representation of juveniles, including numbers of youth appearing without counsel; spending on juvenile defense, with adequate safeguards in place to ensure confidentiality; and defender caseloads.
- Encourage appropriate citizen groups to observe court proceedings in order to support effective representation of juveniles.

ENDNOTES

1. All quotations were obtained from on-site interviews with lawyers and their clients. Names have been changed to protect their identities.
2. This lack of basic fairness is not confined to urban areas. Attorneys who represent juveniles in rural areas speak of the problems of "rurality". While these attorneys may not have the high caseloads of their urban counterparts, their clients may be scattered over several counties, meaning that sheer distance prohibits frequent contact between attorneys and clients. Attorneys in rural areas have had to drive several hundred miles to a remote location and spend the night, simply to be able to represent a client in a 20-minute hearing the next day.
3. Although juvenile arrests for violent crimes increased by 45% between 1982 and 1992, the overall arrest rates for juvenile crimes generally has decreased, and arrest statistics may exaggerate the problem of youth violence. Juveniles often commit crimes in groups, which may inflate the number of arrests. National victimization studies, which report the number of crimes committed, indicate that "the nation's overall violent and nonviolent crime rates have actually fallen over the last 20 years." MICHAEL JONES & BARRY KRISBERG, NATIONAL COUNCIL ON CRIME AND DELINQUENCY, IMAGES AND REALITY: JUVENILE CRIME, YOUTH VIOLENCE AND PUBLIC POLICY 2 (June 1994). In one area — use of firearms — there has been a dramatic increase: between 1985 and 1992 the handgun homicide rate for teenagers nearly tripled. *Id.* at 17. *See also* PETER W. GREENWOOD & FRANKLIN E. ZIMRING, ONE MORE CHANCE: THE PURSUIT OF PRIMARY INTERVENTION STRATEGIES FOR CHRONIC JUVENILE OFFENDERS 2 (May 1995); *see generally* Jeffrey A. Butts, *Offenders in Juvenile Court 1992,* JUV. JUST. BULL. (Office of Juvenile Justice and Delinquency Prevention, U.S. Dep't of Justice) Oct. 1994 at 5–6.
4. OFFICE OF JUVENILE JUSTICE AND DELINQUENCY PREVENTION, U.S. DEP'T OF JUSTICE, JUVENILE OFFENDERS AND VICTIMS: A FOCUS ON VIOLENCE (May 1995). Linda Roeder, *Special Report: Juveniles in Adult Court,* 20 CHILD PROTECTION REP. 171–176 (Oct. 1994); AMERICAN BAR ASSOCIATION PRESIDENTIAL WORKING GROUP ON THE UNMET NEEDS OF CHILDREN AND THEIR FAMILIES, AMERICA'S CHILDREN AT RISK: A NATIONAL AGENDA FOR LEGAL ACTION (1993) [hereinafter AMERICA'S CHILDREN AT RISK].
5. JONES, *supra* note 3, at 34–35; *see generally* Butts, *supra* note 3, at 2, 8.
6. OFFICE OF JUVENILE JUSTICE AND DELINQUENCY PREVENTION, U.S. DEP'T OF JUSTICE, CONDITIONS OF CONFINEMENT: JUVENILE DETENTION AND CORRECTIONS FACILITIES, RESEARCH SUMMARY 7–13 (Feb. l994).
7. AMERICA'S CHILDREN AT RISK, *supra* note 4, at 61–62. Juvenile justice experts have also raised concerns that current trends in lowering the age at which juveniles can be tried as adults will further disadvantage minority juveniles; in fact, a recent study of prosecutor selection of cases to be transferred to adult court in Texas has revealed significant racial disparities, even when offenses and prior court referrals were taken into account. Robert O. Dawson, *An Empirical Study of Kent Style Juvenile Transfers to Criminal Court,* 23 ST. MARY'S L. J. 975, 998–1001 (1992).

    The imposition of the death penalty for crimes committed by juveniles is no less racially-biased; of thirty-three death sentences in force in 1993, 61% were for minorities, 52% African-American and 9% Hispanic-American. Coramae Richey Mann, *A Minority View of Juvenile Justice,* 51 WASH. & LEE L. REV. 465, 475 (1994) (citing Victor L. Streib, *The Juvenile Death Penalty Today: Present Death Row Inmates Under Juvenile Death Sentences and Death Sentences and Execution for Juvenile Crimes January 1, 1973 to December 31, 1993* (May 18, 1993)).
8. 387 U.S. l (1967).

9. The first challenge in conducting the national survey of juvenile defenders was compiling a list of defender offices, children's law centers, and law schools with clinical programs that handle juvenile delinquency cases. There are no comprehensive national or regional directories that list public and private attorneys who engage in juvenile defense practice.

    The list of defender offices was compiled from a variety of sources. The project team created a sampling frame using an "opportunistic snowball" approach. First, to target the survey, the team contacted the Administrative Office of the Court in every state to obtain information about the public defender and court appointment system. Next, the team used the National Legal Aid and Defender Association's directory to contact defender offices in every state. The project team then held focus group meetings at national conferences to obtain suggestions about compiling the list of juvenile defenders. The team also polled the 150 members of the American Bar Association's Juvenile Justice Committee to seek their advice and suggestions. Finally, the team used the American Association of Law School's directory to identify clinical law school programs that include delinquency cases.

    From these sources, the project team mailed surveys to approximately 260 public defender's offices, 162 contract attorneys, 53 law schools and 33 children's law centers. Every respondent who received a survey was asked to pass the survey on to a colleague, if he or she was not the appropriate person to complete it. To improve the response rate, the project team contacted offices that failed to return the survey and conducted phone interviews with them.

10. The surveys consisted of both open-ended and closed-ended questions to learn about the types of services defenders provide to juveniles and the quality of those services. The closed-ended questions allowed the compilation of descriptive statistics while the open-ended questions helped to clarify responses and provide details about lawyers' work. The project team obtained a wealth of data by combining these two formats. While the surveys were tailored for each category of respondent (public defender, appointed counsel, law school clinical program, and children's law center), common questions were included whenever possible to enable comparisons of responses among those engaged in different types of juvenile defense practice.

11. IJA/ABA JUVENILE JUSTICE STANDARDS (1980). In the early 1980's, the ABA House of Delegates adopted twenty volumes of Juvenile Justice Standards as official Association policy. The Standards were drafted under the auspices of a Joint Commission with representatives of the Institute of Judicial Administration, American Bar Association, and dozens of juvenile justice experts.

12. 387 U.S. 1 (1967).

13. *Id.* at 28.

14. *Id.* at 36.

15. *Id.* at 39 n.65 (quoting PRESIDENT'S COMMISSION ON LAW ENFORCEMENT AND THE ADMINISTRATION OF JUSTICE, THE CHALLENGE OF CRIME IN A FREE SOCIETY 86–87 (1967)).

16. Juvenile Justice and Delinquency Prevention Act of 1974, Pub. L. 93–415, 88 Stat. 1141 (codified in sections of 5, 18 & 42 U.S.C.).

17. 42 U.S.C. § 5601(a)(2).

18. NATIONAL ADVISORY COMMITTEE FOR JUVENILE JUSTICE AND DELINQUENCY PREVENTION, STANDARDS FOR THE ADMINISTRATION OF JUVENILE JUSTICE (1980).

19. *Id.* at Standard 3.132.

20. IJA/ABA JUVENILE JUSTICE STANDARDS, STANDARDS RELATING TO COUNSEL FOR PRIVATE PARTIES (1980) [hereinafter STANDARDS ON COUNSEL FOR PRIVATE PARTIES]; *see also* Howard A. Davidson, *The Child's Right To Be Heard and Represented in Juvenile Proceedings*, 18 PEPP. L. REV. 255, 265–66 (1991).

21. AMERICA'S CHILDREN AT RISK, *supra* note 4, at 60.

22. *Id.*

23. *Id.* at 60–68.

24. Barry C. Feld, *In re Gault Revisited: A Cross-State Comparison of the Right to Counsel in Juvenile Court*, 34 CRIME & DELINQ. 393 (1988) [hereinafter Feld, *Cross-State*

Comparison]; Barry C. Feld, *The Right to Counsel in Juvenile Court: An Empirical Study of When Lawyers Appear and the Difference They Make*, 79 J. CRIM. L. & CRIMINOLOGY 1185 (1989) [hereinafter Feld, *When Lawyers Appear*]; Barry C. Feld, *Punitive Juvenile Court and the Quality of Procedural Justice: Disjunctions Between Rhetoric and Reality*, 36 CRIME & DELINQ. 443 (1990) [hereinafter Feld, *Punitive Juvenile Court*]; Barry C. Feld, *Justice By Geography: Urban, Suburban, and Rural Variations in Juvenile Justice Administration*, 82 J. CRIM. L. & CRIMINOLOGY 156 (1991) [hereinafter Feld, *Justice By Geography*]; BARRY C. FELD, JUSTICE FOR CHILDREN: THE RIGHT TO COUNSEL AND THE JUVENILE COURTS (1993) [HEREINAFTER FELD, JUSTICE FOR CHILDREN].

25. Feld, *When Lawyers Appear, supra* note 24, at 1199; FELD, JUSTICE FOR CHILDREN, *supra* note 24, at 27.

26. Feld, *Cross-State Comparison, supra* note 24, at 416; FELD, JUSTICE FOR CHILDREN, *supra* note 24, at 72.

27. Feld, *When Lawyers Appear, supra* note 24, at 1320; FELD, JUSTICE FOR CHILDREN, *supra* note 24, at 81.

28. Feld, *Justice By Geography, supra* note 24, at 206–10; FELD, JUSTICE FOR CHILDREN, *supra* note 24, at 181–88.

29. FELD, JUSTICE FOR CHILDREN, *supra* note 24, at 54–55. Feld found, too, that the likelihood that a child will receive legal representation also increased if there had been prior referrals for delinquent behavior, there were multiple charges against the child, or the child was detained. In addition, there was a significant positive correlation between rate of representation and dispositions involving out-of-home placement or secure confinement. *Id.* at 58–60, 62–64, & 69–70.

30. Feld, *When Lawyers Appear, supra* note 24, at 1239–40; Feld, *Punitive Juvenile Court, supra* note 24, at 443 FELD, JUSTICE FOR CHILDREN, *supra* note 24, at 102.

31. John M. Stuart, *Right to Counsel: The Unkept Promise to Our Juvenile Accused*, 48 BENCH & B. MINN. 27 (Aug. 1991); *see* FELD, JUSTICE FOR CHILDREN, *supra* note 24, at 28.

32. *See generally* Arkansas Advocates for Children and Families, *Due Process Rights and Legal Procedures in Arkansas' Juvenile Courts*, OJJDP Grant #80-JS-AX-0026 (1983); Paula J. Casey, *Arkansas Juvenile Courts: Do Lay Judges Satisfy Due Process in Delinquency Cases?*, 6 U. ARK. LITTLE ROCK L.J. 501 (1983); Steven H. Clark & Gary G. Koch, *Juvenile Court: Therapy or Crime Control, and Do Lawyers Make a Difference?*, 14 L. & SOC'Y REV. 263 (1980) (North Carolina); Paul Marcotte, *Criminal Kids*, 76 A.B.A. J. 61 (Apr. 1990) (discussing Feld and others); James D. Walter & Susan A. Ostrander, *An Observational Study of a Juvenile Court*, 33 Juv. & Fam. Ct. J 53 (1982); BRUCE G. DEW, A STUDY OF DEFENSE SERVICES FOR INDIGENT JUVENILE DEFENDANTS IN SOUTH CAROLINA: ANALYSIS AND RECOMMENDATIONS; THE SPANGENBERG GROUP, STUDY OF THE INDIGENT DEFENDER SYSTEM IN LOUISIANA: FINAL REPORT (Mar. 12, 1992); TENNESSEE COMMISSION ON CHILDREN AND YOUTH, CHILDREN'S PLAN EVALUATION REPORT (Nov. 1994); REPORT OF THE JUVENILE REPRESENTATION STUDY COMMITTEE TO THE MINNESOTA SUPREME COURT (June 5, 1990).

33. *See generally* Thomas C. Castellano, *The Justice Model in the Juvenile Justice System: Washington State's Experience*, 8 L. & POL'Y 488 (1986); Janet Ainsworth, *Re-Imagining Childhood and Reconstructing the Legal Order: The Case for Abolishing the Juvenile Court*, 69 N.C. L. REV. 1083 (1991) (discussing Feld's Minnesota work and other surveys); ROBERT L. BING, SCOTT H. DECKER, & KIMBERLY L. KAUPF, CENTER FOR METROPOLITAN STUDIES, UNIVERSITY OF MISSOURI - ST. LOUIS, AN ANALYSIS OF APPARENT DISPARITIES IN THE HANDLING OF BLACK YOUTH WITHIN MISSOURI'S JUVENILE JUSTICE SYSTEMS (Nov. 1990); MISSOURI DEPARTMENT OF PUBLIC SAFETY AND MISSOURI JUVENILE JUSTICE ADVISORY GROUP, THE STATE OF JUVENILE JUSTICE: ISSUES AND PRIORITIES FOR MISSOURI'S JUVENILE JUSTICE SYSTEM (1994).

34. M.A. BORTNER, INSIDE A JUVENILE COURT: THE TARNISHED IDEAL OF INDIVIDUALIZED JUSTICE 136 (1982); FELD, JUSTICE FOR CHILDREN, *supra* note 24, at 31–32.

35. Erin M. Smith, *In a Child's Best Interests: Juvenile Status Offenders Deserve Procedural Due Process*, 10 L. & INEQUALITY 253, at 259–60 (1992); Criminal Justice

Statistical Analysis Center, *How Today's Juvenile Justice Trends Have Affected Policy* (1984).

36. FELD, JUSTICE FOR CHILDREN, *supra* note 24, at 28. Feld found that privately retained attorneys are more likely to appear in felony cases and cases involving offenses against the person, but they still appear in only a small percentage of delinquency cases. *Id.* at 56.
37. Feld, *Cross-State Comparison, supra* note 24, at 395; Feld, *When Lawyers Appear, supra* note 24, at 1200–01; FELD, JUSTICE FOR CHILDREN, *supra* note 24, at 28–32.
38. AMERICA'S CHILDREN AT RISK, *supra* note 4, at 60.
39. Feld, *Justice by Geography, supra* note 24, at 186; Feld, *When Lawyers Appear, supra* note 24, at 1219; FELD, JUSTICE FOR CHILDREN, *supra* note 24, at 82, 184.
40. JANE KNITZER & MERRIL SOBIE, NEW YORK STATE BAR ASSOCIATION, LAW GUARDIANS IN NEW YORK STATE: A STUDY OF THE LEGAL REPRESENTATION OF CHILDREN 4–5 (1984).
41. Panel lawyers consisted of a list of attorneys willing to represent children on a per case basis. It was estimated that 2,300 panel attorneys existed at the time of the study. They were paid $25 an hour for in court activities and $15 an hour for out of court activities. *Id.* at 2–3. For a profile of panel attorneys, *see generally id.* at 19–54.
42. *Id.* at 6–7.
43. BARBARA FLICKER, INSTITUTE OF JUDICIAL ADMINISTRATION, PROVIDING COUNSEL FOR ACCUSED JUVENILES 5–6 (June 1983).
44. DEW, *supra* note 32, at 13–14, 19–35; THE ILLINOIS SUPREME COURT SPECIAL COMMISSION ON THE ADMINISTRATION OF JUSTICE: FINAL REPORT, PART II 7–11 (Dec. 1993); SPANGENBERG, *supra* note 32, at 2–7; *see generally* ROBERT F. MUSE, ET AL., REPORT OF A SPECIAL COMMITTEE OF THE DISTRICT OF COLUMBIA BAR REGARDING COURT APPOINTMENT OF COUNSEL PROGRAMS IN THE SUPERIOR COURT (Dec. 21, 1993).
45. *See generally* Judge Leonard P. Edwards, *A Comprehensive Approach to the Representation of Children: The Child Advocacy Coordinating Council,* 27 FAM. L. Q. 417 (1993).
46. *Id.* at 418–20; *see also* M. FINKELSTEIN, ET. AL., PROSECUTION IN THE JUVENILE COURTS AND GUIDELINES FOR THE FUTURE 40–42 (1973).
47. Xavier G. Velasco, et. al., THE JUVENILE COURT IN THEORY AND IN OPERATION, 4 CHI. B. ASS'N. REC. 26, 27 (1990).
48. Ainsworth, *supra* note 33, at 1128 n. 305.
49. BORTNER, *supra* note 34, at 141.
50. DEW, *supra* note 32, at 25–26; ILLINOIS SUPREME COURT SPECIAL COMMISSION, *supra* note 44, at 7–11.
51. Richard A. Lawrence, *The Role of Legal Counsel in Juvenile's Understanding of Their Rights,* 34 JUV. & FAM. CT. J. 49, 57 (Winter 1983–84); *see generally* KNITZER, *supra* note 40.
52. BORTNER, *supra* note 34, at 141; *see also* DEW, *supra* note 32, at 17–19.
53. Robert E. Shepherd, Jr. & Adrienne Volenik, *Juvenile Justice,* 2 CRIM. JUST. 33 (Fall 1987).
54. BORTNER, *supra* note 34, at 136–39.
55. Ainsworth, *supra* note 33, at 1127; KNITZER, *supra* note 40, at 131–33; FINKELSTEIN, *supra* note 46, at 41–42.
56. Jan C. Costello, *Ethical Issues in Representing Juvenile Clients: A Review of the IJA/ABA Standards on Representing Private Parties,* 10 N.M. L. REV. 255, 263–64 (1980) (prepared under OJJDP grant #78-JS-AX-003).
57. BORTNER, *supra* note 34, at 136–37; Ainsworth, *supra* note 33, at 1129–30.
58. Regina Huerter & Bonnie Saltzman, *What Do They Think? The Delinquency Court Process in Colorado as Viewed by the Youth,* 69 DENV. U. L. REV. 345, 354 (1992).
59. Clark, *supra* note 32, at 268; BORTNER, *supra* note 34, at 136–37; FLICKER, *supra* note 43, at 3–4; Feld, *When Lawyers Appear, supra* note 24, at 1331; FELD, JUSTICE FOR CHILDREN, *supra* note 24, at 254–55; Ainsworth, *supra* note 33, at 1128–29; *see generally* Muse, *supra* note 44.
60. Ainsworth, *supra* note 33, at 1129.

61. For an excellent and exhaustive discussion of the role of counsel in delinquency proceedings, see RANDY HERTZ, ET AL., AMERICAN LAW INSTITUTE / AMERICAN BAR ASSOCIATION, COMMITTEE ON CONTINUING PROFESSIONAL EDUCATION, TRIAL MANUAL FOR DEFENSE ATTORNEYS IN JUVENILE COURT v. 1–2 (1991).
62. *Id.* at 36–37.
63. *Id.* at 36.
64. STANDARDS ON COUNSEL FOR PRIVATE PARTIES, *supra* note 20, at Standard 3.3(a) commentary at 90.
65. Juvenile courts processed 1,471,200 delinquency cases in the United States in 1992. Jeffrey A. Butts, *Delinquency Cases in Juvenile Court 1992*, Fact Sheet #18 (Office of Juvenile Justice and Delinquency Prevention, U.S. Dep't of Justice) July 1994 at 1.
66. The police have wide discretion to warn and release youths without entering formal charges. In some communities, police can refer youth directly to social service agencies.
67. STANDARDS ON COUNSEL FOR PRIVATE PARTIES, *supra* note 20, at Standard 4.1.
68. For example, looking at data on all youth arrested during 1992 for offenses against persons, of those who were detained, 23.5% were ultimately placed out-of-home, while only 5.4% of those not detained were placed out-of-home. Butts, *supra* note 3.
69. IJA/ABA JUVENILE JUSTICE STANDARDS, STANDARDS RELATING TO PRETRIAL COURT PROCEEDINGS Standard 6.1(a) (1980) [hereinafter STANDARDS ON PRETRIAL COURT PROCEEDINGS].
70. STANDARDS ON COUNSEL FOR PRIVATE PARTIES, *supra* note 20, at Standard 4.2(a).
71. *Id.* at Standard 4.3.
72. *Id.*
73. *Id.* at Standard 4.3(b).
74. *Id.* at Standard 2.3(ii).
75. During the pretrial period counsel should be aware of the availability of extraordinary writs. A habeas corpus petition may be required for a client who is being held beyond the allowable statutory period, or a mandamus petition may be required when a judge refuses to release a client who has a statutory or constitutional right to be released. The client may also require legal assistance in cases that are not directly related to the criminal case. Counsel should help the client with such matters, such as receiving educational services and benefits, at least to the extent of referring the client to other attorneys who practice in that area.
76. This is the procedure endorsed by the IJA/ABA Juvenile Justice Standards. *See* IJA/ABA JUVENILE JUSTICE STANDARDS, STANDARDS RELATING TO TRANSFER BETWEEN COURTS Standard 2.3(E) (1980); STANDARDS ON COUNSEL FOR PRIVATE PARTIES, *supra* note 20, at Standard 8.1.
77. CAL. WELF. & INST. CODE § 1731.5 (West 1995).
78. MINN. STAT. § 260.115 (1)(1994).
79. *See* McKeiver v. Pennsylvania, 403 U.S. 528 (1971).
80. There are two kinds of pleas. One involves an admission by the child to particular charges in return for the state's agreement to recommend to the court a specific disposition (such as probation, or commitment to a residential treatment facility). There is also an "open plea," in which the youth admits to an offense, the prosecution makes no recommendation, and disposition is left completely to the discretion of the court.
81. IJA/ABA JUVENILE JUSTICE STANDARDS, STANDARDS RELATING TO ADJUDICATION Standard 3.1(a) (1980). The Standards further state that in determining whether the respondent has the mental capacity to enter a plea admitting an allegation of the petition, the juvenile court should inquire into, among other factors:

> (1) the respondent's chronological age; (2) the respondent's present grade level in school or the highest grade level achieved while in school; (3) whether the respondent can read

and write; and (4) whether the respondent has ever been diagnosed or treated for mental illness or mental retardation.

Id. at Standard 3.1(b)(1–4).

82. Margaret Beyer, *The Use of Evaluations in Family Court*, 5 ABA Juv. and Ch. Welf. Rptr. 170 (1987).
83. IJA/ABA Juvenile Justice Standards, Standards Relating to Disposition Standard 2.1 (1980) [hereinafter Standards on Disposition].
84. *Id.* at Standard 2.2.
85. Standards on Counsel for Private Parties, *supra* note 20, at Standard 10.1.
86. *Id.* at Standard 10.5.
87. *Id.* at Standard 2.3.
88. *Id.* at Standard 10.3(b).
89. Morales v. Turman, 326 F. Supp. 677 (E.D. Tex. 1971), *aff'd*, 364 F. Supp. 166 (E.D. Tex. 1973), 383 F. Supp. 53 (E.D. Tex. 1974), *rev'd and remanded*, 535 F.2d 864 (5th Cir. 1976).
90. Mark Soler, et al., Representing the Child Client 1.55–62 (Matthew Bender 1987).
91. *Id.* at 2.9–12.
92. *Id.* at 2.101–103.
93. *Id.* at 2.79–81.
94. *Id.* at 2.96–100.
95. Soler, *supra* note 90, at 2.92–96.
96. *Id.* at 2.15–21.
97. *Id.* at 2.56–62.
98. *Id.* at 2.53–56.
99. *Id.* at 2.62–64.
100. Soler, *supra* note 90, at 2.64–66.
101. Standards on Counsel for Private Parties, *supra* note 20, commentary to Standard 2.3.
102. Richard Klein & Robert Spangenberg, American Bar Association Section of Criminal Justice, Ad Hoc Committee on the Indigent Defense Crisis, The Indigent Defense Crisis (1993).
103. Kent v. United States, 383 U.S. 541 (1966).
104. In re Gault, 387 U.S. 1 (1967).
105. Standards on Pretrial Court Proceedings, *supra* note 69, at Standard 6; IJA/ABA Juvenile Justice Standards, Standards Relating to Juvenile Probation Function Standard 2.13 (1980).
106. See Table PD-5. The statistics of court-appointed attorneys responding were again almost identical. See Table PA-5.
107. Finkelstein, *supra* note 46, at 51–53; Ainsworth, *supra* note 33, at 1127–28; *see generally* Knitzer *supra* note 40; *Cf.* Muse, *supra* note 44.
108. *See generally* Costello, *supra* note 56; John L. Roche, *Juvenile Court Dispositional Alternatives: Imposing a Duty on the Defense*, 27 Santa Clara L. Rev. 279 (1987); Judge Edwards, *supra* note 45.
109. Bortner, *supra* note 34, at 140–42; Finkelstein, *supra* note 46, at 54.
110. Feld, Justice for Children, *supra* note 24, at 210. Feld is quick to urge caution in interpreting his data. He suggests that the correlation between the type of lawyer representing the child and the severity of sentencing may reflect the ability of retained attorneys to act more independently than public attorneys, but having retained counsel also signals to the court the relative affluence of the family and concomitant capacity to show the family's sponsorship of the child so as to justify a more lenient sentence. However, public attorneys may reap other benefits because of ongoing involvement in the courts: Feld found that public attorneys have a better chance of having the original charges reduced to a "lesser included" or related offense than retained counsel. *Id.* at 220–21.
111. Standards for the Administration of Juvenile Justice: Report of the National Advisory Committee for Juvenile Justice and Delinquency Prevention, Standard 1.424 (1980).

112. A study of Pennsylvania appeals by youth whose dispositions led to out-of-home placement found that there were in 1990 only 35 appeals of juvenile cases, when 3,678 youth were committed to delinquency institutions. In contrast, 3,150 adults took appeals, while 28,957 received jail or prison sentences. There were no appeals taken in 54 of Pennsylvania's 67 counties. In Allegheny County, where 488 adult appeals were filed in 1990, only one juvenile appeal was filed. In Philadelphia County, where there were 912 adult appeals, only 17 juveniles took appeals. Donald J. Harris, *Due Process v. Helping Kids in Trouble: Implementing the Right to Appeal from Adjudications of Delinquency in Pennsylvania*, 98 DICK. L. REV. 209, 234–35 (Winter 1994). It should be noted that the data emerging from this survey and from the Pennsylvania study merely shows the percentage of cases appealed. It does not provide any information about the quality of the appellate work being done.
113. For example, the Juvenile Defender Unit of the Dade County Public Defender's Office in Miami, Florida has acknowledged the debilitating effect crushing caseloads have on both the quality of representation and attorney morale. With the support of the Public Defender, the supervisor of the Juvenile Unit has been able to put in place a number of innovations to ease caseload burdens and provide holistic legal services, including a staff team of social workers that partner up with the lawyers to work on complex cases. In addition, through advocacy and hard work, the Public Defender was able to obtain additional funds from the county to supplement the states' appropriation so that more juvenile defenders could be hired.
114. John L. v. Adams, 750 F. Supp. 288 (M.D. Tenn. 1990).
115. The Ohio State Public Defender in Columbus teamed up with the Department of Youth Services to develop a project that would provide better access to legal representation for youth who had been committed to the Department. The statewide project began in 1994.
116. See Juvenile Special Defense Unit of the Defender Association of Pennsylvania located in Philadelphia, PA., and the Mandel Legal Aid Clinic associated with the University of Chicago Law School in Chicago, IL.
117. Early intervention is the hallmark of the Neighborhood Defender Services of Harlem. This demonstration project, created in 1990 by the Vera Institute, is a community-based model that uses a team approach, provides vertical representation, and can sometimes dispose of the case at the initial appearance because of early intervention.
118. See Juvenile Rights Division of the New York Legal Aid Society, New York, New York, or the Public Defender Service of the District of Columbia located in Washington DC.
119. See Public Defender Service in the District of Columbia, Washington, DC.
120. See Neighborhood Defender Service of Harlem, New York, New York.
121. See for example, Public Defender Service of the District of Columbia, Washington, DC; Youth Advocacy Project in Roxbury, Massachusetts; Juvenile Rights Division of the New York Legal Aid Society in New York City; or Juvenile Special Defense Unit of the Defender Association of Philadelphia, PA.
122. The Detention Response Unit of the Office of the Public Defender, State of Maryland, Baltimore, MD.
123. TEAMCHILD, a joint project of the Seattle/King County Public Defender Association and Evergreen Legal Services, 1995.
124. For that reason, the data collected from the law clinics regarding their cases and the quality of representation is not very useful.

For information about practice and policy
issues related to juvenile defense
please contact:

National Juvenile Defender Center
1350 Connecticut Avenue, NW
Washington, DC 20036
(202) 452-0010
www.njdc.info